JAMS AND PRESERVES

more than 100 jam, chutney,
and preserve recipes

THUNDER BAY
P·R·E·S·S

San Diego, California

CONTENTS

Making jams and preserves

How good it is to be able to eat fresh cherry jam on biscuit in midwinter, or spicy, vegetable-laden chutneys with a barbecue in the height of summer. Preserving is a culinary technique that's both easy and satisfying to learn, and it rewards us with sweet and savory produce to enjoy year-round.

For centuries, jams, preserves, chutneys, and pickles have been made to ensure a regular food supply during colder and leaner times. They are best made at the peak of the season when the fruit and vegetables are flavorsome, plentiful, and inexpensive.

WHICH FRUIT TO CHOOSE

When making jams, preserves, chutneys, or pickles, it is essential to use good-quality fruits and vegetables to obtain the best results. Always choose fruit that is firm and just ripe, and without any blemishes or bruises. Overripe fruit will lack the pectin needed to set the preserve. If the fruit is quite ripe, add about 10 percent of underripe fruit to increase the pectin to the amount needed to set the preserve.

SUGAR and PECTIN

When making jams and jellies, the balance of the acid in the fruit, the sugar, and the pectin will all play a part in the final firmness and flavor of the preserve. Sugar is not just used as a sweetener when making jams and jellies. It is also a preservative when used in a high concentration, inhibiting the development and growth of micro-organisms. To reach a high enough concentration, ¾–1 cup of sugar must be used per 1 cup of fruit.

Sugar is also a setting agent and aids the setting process in jams and jellies that would not set without a store-bought setting agent.

Pectin is found in the skin, flesh, and seeds of most fruits in varying degrees. It is particularly high in citrus pith and apple skin. Some fruits are quite low in pectin or have none at all and need the addition of pectin-containing fruit or juice, or store-bought setting agents, to help them set.

The acid level of the fruit is also important, because it acts as a preservative and setting agent. If low, acid levels can be supplemented with the addition of lemon juice or by combining several fruits in the one recipe. A store-bought setting agent isn't always needed, and if the preserve sets when tested it may not be necessary to add it at all.

Successful jams and preserves require an even balance of pectin and acid. The chart below states the levels of pectin and acid found in fruits that are commonly used in jams and preserves.

TESTING FOR PECTIN

If you are not sure how much pectin is in the fruit you want to use for your jelly, place 2 teaspoons

of denatured alcohol in a small bowl and then gently add 1 teaspoon of the strained fruit mixture and stir gently. If there is enough pectin present to set the jelly, clots should form into one large lump. If they form smaller lumps, the mixture will need to be reduced some more or you will need to add some lemon juice. If the mixture is then still not setting, you may need to use a store-bought setting agent. Follow the packet instructions.

SUGAR

You will notice that all our sweet preserve recipes call for warmed sugar. While warming the sugar before adding it to the pan is not absolutely imperative in a recipe and won't affect the final outcome, it does speed up the dissolving process. The sugar dissolves more quickly and, because it is warm, will not reduce the temperature of the fruit mixture as much as if you had added cold sugar. To warm sugar, spread it in an even layer in a deep-sided baking pan and warm in an oven preheated to 300°F for 10–15 minutes, or until warmed through. Do not overheat the sugar or it will start to lump together. To make sure this

PECTIN AND ACID LEVELS IN FRUITS

HIGH PECTIN	MEDIUM PECTIN	LOW PECTIN	HIGH ACID	LOW ACID
black currants	apricots	bananas	blackberries (early)	apricots
citrus fruits	blackberries (early)	blackberries (late)	black currants	figs
cooking apples	eating apples	boysenberries	cherries	kiwifruit
grapes	loganberries	cherries	citrus fruits	mangoes
plums	mulberries	figs	green apples	canteloupes
(some varieties)	peaches	guava	pineapple	passion fruit
quinces	pears	canteloupes	plums	pears
red currants	raspberries	nectarines	raspberries (early)	quinces
	rhubarb	passion fruit	red currants	rhubarb
	strawberries	pineapple		strawberries
				sweet apples

doesn't happen, stir the sugar once or twice while it is warming up. To save time, warm the sugar while you are cooking the fruit.

Do not add the sugar until the fruit has softened. If sugar is added before the fruit is fully soft, it will stay firm. Regular granulated sugar is used in our jam, jelly, and preserve recipes unless otherwise specified. Superfine sugar is used in some recipes for quicker dissolving and better clarity. Brown sugar is used mostly in chutneys, pickles, and relishes to enhance the flavors and give a deeper, rich color.

EQUIPMENT

Good-quality, large, heavy-bottomed stainless steel or enamel pans are one of the most important pieces of equipment you can have when making jams and preserves. And, if you are going to make large amounts on a regular basis, it's well worth buying special preserving pans.

Sugar thermometers are a very helpful gauge for temperatures. It is crucial, when bottling and sealing your preserve, that the temperature stays at or above 185°F. This will prevent the growth of potentially harmful bacteria. If you don't have a sugar thermometer, make sure you seal your preserve in its jar as soon as it is ready. You can also use your thermometer to test whether your preserve has reached setting point This generally occurs once the mixture has reached 220°F. However we haven't used this method much in this book, relying more on testing on a saucer with the wrinkle method.

Jam funnels make filling jars a little easier without the jam dripping down the sides. Large and small heatproof pitchers are essential for pouring and measuring. A metal skimmer or metal spoon is ideal for removing scum from the surface of the jam or preserve. Ladles are often used to transfer cooked preserves to jars. Wooden spoons are needed for stirring, and, of course, a pastry brush to clean down the sides of the pan.

Cheesecloth is used throughout this book both to drain liquids and to hold seeds and peel in a secure bundle. Cheesecloth can be purchased at kitchenware or fabric stores. Alternatively, you can use a clean dish towel. When you are straining mixtures such as jellies, ensure that the material is

DEFINITIONS

JAM—made from small pieces of fruit and sugar, cooked to a thick, spreadable consistency.

PRESERVE—whole fruits preserved in a heavy, sugar-based syrup.

CONSERVE—whole or large pieces of fruit cooked with sugar until thick.

JELLY—made from the strained juice of cooked fruits, and sugar. Generally clear, but can contain small pieces of the original fruit.

MARMALADE—sliced, cooked citrus fruits, suspended in a sweet, thick jam mixture.

FRUIT PASTE—strained, cooked fruit, cooked to a thick paste with sugar and cut into pieces when cold.

FRUIT CURD—thick, spreadable, creamy mixture made with juice, fruit purée, and sometimes citrus peel, combined with sugar, eggs, and butter and cooked until thick.

PICKLE—vegetables, or sometimes fruit, pickled in vinegar with sugar, salt, and spices.

CHUTNEY—vegetables and/or fruit cooked with vinegar, sugar, and spices to a thick consistency.

RELISH—salted cooked vegetables in a sugar, spice, and vinegar-based sauce, which is thickened toward the end of cooking.

just damp so that it won't absorb too much of the liquid.

Before starting to cook your jam or preserve, ensure your equipment has been carefully washed in hot, soapy water and the jars you intend to use are thoroughly clean. Always make sure you have enough clean jars ready for when you have a pan full of boiling jam ready to bottle. The best way to ensure that jars are spotlessly clean is to preheat the oven to 250°F. Thoroughly wash the jars and lids in hot, soapy water (or preferably in a dishwasher) and rinse well with hot water. Put the jars on cookie sheets and place them in the oven for 20 minutes, or until you are ready to use them. They must be dried fully in the oven.

HOW IT ALL WORKS

Whether you are making jams, preserves, jellies, pickles, chutneys, or relishes, the method to use is essentially the same. Obviously, sweet jams, preserves, and jellies require a lot more sugar than the savory pickles, chutneys, and relishes. They are also self-setting in that the mixture thickens on cooling to an easily spreadable consistency.

JAMS

Try not to cook too much jam all in one quantity. Do not use more than 4 pounds fruit in a recipe at a time. You also need to make sure that your pan is large enough. Ideally, the mixture should be no more than 2 inches deep after the sugar has been added. Chutneys and pickles can be cooked in larger quantities, but remember that the more mixture you have in the pan, then the longer the cooking time. Jellies are generally cooked in smaller quantities.

Wash and dry the fruit well to remove any dirt. If you are using citrus fruits such as oranges or grapefruit, gently scrub the fruit with a soft bristle brush under warm running water to remove the wax coating. Remove any stalks from berries and cut away any damaged or bruised pieces of fruit (which you shouldn't have if you'd chosen your fruit carefully in the beginning). Cut up the fruit according to the recipe and place it into your pan to soften. Be aware that some recipes require the fruit to be soaked overnight. Reserved seeds and extra skin or fruit are used in many recipes in this book, particularly lemon seeds and peel. These are wrapped in a square of cheesecloth and can either be soaked overnight with the fruit, and then cooked with the fruit, as with marmalade, or simply added to the pan and cooked with the jam or preserve. For easy retrieval of the cheesecloth bag, attach a long piece of string to the bag and tie it to the handle of the pan. The remaining ingredients are added according to each individual recipe.

The wrinkle test is a quick and easy way to see if jam has reached its setting point.

If the jam is not setting, cook a little longer and test again, using the second chilled plate.

If the jam is overcooked, it will be much thicker and darker than it should be.

> *"I value my garden more for being full of blackbirds than of cherries, and very frankly give them fruit for their songs."*
>
> — *Joseph Addison*

Bring the mixture to a boil, then reduce the heat and simmer for the specified time until the fruit is tender. Then add the required amount of sugar. Remove any scum or foam from the top of the jam or preserve throughout the cooking process. The scum that forms on the top of the mixture is usually any impurities or dirt present on the fruit or sugar. Stir over the heat, without boiling, until all the sugar has dissolved. Brush the side of the pan with a pastry brush dipped in water, to dissolve any excess sugar crystals that can sometimes cause jams to crystallize toward the end of cooking. If the jam does crystallize, add 1–2 tablespoons of lemon juice and gently reheat. Be aware that this may change the taste slightly. Once all the sugar has dissolved, boil the mixture rapidly for the required time. Stir the jam often while it is cooking to speed up the cooking process and ensure that it does not stick to the bottom of the pan. After the specified cooking time is completed, or when the jam or preserve looks thick and syrupy, the mixture should fall from a wooden spoon heavily with 3 or 4 drops joining in a sheet as they drop. This means that the jam or preserve has reached its setting point.

Cooking times vary greatly between recipes, depending on pan sizes, the fruit used, the time of year, and if the fruit is in season, among other reasons. Therefore, it's necessary to test for setting point, sometimes up to 10 minutes before the stated time, to make sure the jam or preserve is ready to be bottled. Do not rely entirely on the times stated. Remove the pan from the heat, place 1 teaspoon of the jam on one of the cold plates and place it in the freezer for about 30 seconds, or until the jam has cooled to room temperature. Gently push through the jam with the tip of your finger. There should be a skin on top of the jam which should wrinkle. If it does wrinkle, it's ready. If not, then return the mixture briefly to the heat and try the process again in a few minutes with the second plate.

Immediately spoon or pour the mixture into the warm, clean jars. Pulpier jams tend to have a thicker consistency and jams with large pieces of fruit will need a few minutes standing in the pan

Any scum should be removed from the surface during cooking, using a skimmer.

Brush the side of the pan with a wet pastry brush to remove any sugar crystals.

Setting point has been reached when the jam drops from a spoon in thick sheets.

STICKY SITUATIONS

CRYSTALLIZATION—too much sugar was added to the fruit, and it was not dissolved properly before boiling.

TOUGH FRUIT—the fruit was not cooked long enough before the sugar was added. Fruit does not soften any further once sugar is added.

FRUIT FLOATS—the fruit was not cooked long enough or was not allowed to stand long enough before bottling.

TOO RUNNY—mixture has not set properly. Return it to the pan, bring to a boil again and retest for setting point before bottling.

MOLD—this can start to grow once the jar is opened, if storing in a warm place, or if the mixture was not covered while hot. If caught quickly, mold can be scooped off with a little jam and discarded. Refrigerate the remainder of the jam and eat as soon as possible.

FERMENTATION—mushy, overripe, bruised, or damaged fruits were used in the cooking process, or insufficient sugar was added to the fruit mixture. If you do use less sugar in a recipe, make sure you eat the jam or preserve within a few months because it won't keep as long. The set won't be quite as firm. Keep in the refrigerator after opening

CLOUDINESS—this generally only occurs in jellies, when the jelly strainer bag was squeezed or disturbed while the fruit was dripping through.

before bottling to allow the fruit to be evenly suspended in the mixture.

Don't leave the jam or jelly for too long or it will start to set in the pan. If this does happen, you will need to start all over again. Take care when pouring the preserves into the jars as the mixture is extremely hot. Hold the jar in a dish towel and pour or spoon in the preserve, filling right to the top. If your jars have small openings, it may be easier to first pour the jam into a clean heatproof pitcher then into the jars. You can also use a jam funnel.

Occasionally, you will find you have some air bubbles in the bottles. To remove them, use a thin, clean skewer to help push the mixture to the side and release the bubble to the surface. This technique can be used for all types of preserves. Alternatively, a gentle tap on a cloth on the bench will release some of the air bubbles.

Seal the jars while the mixture is still hot. Turn the jars upside down for 2 minutes, then invert them and let cool. This will ensure the fruit is evenly distributed and the lids are sterilized.

JELLIES

Choose fruits with a good pectin and acid balance for the best results. The fruit is cooked with or without water and then strained overnight in a damp jelly strainer (available from good kitchenware stores) or a damp cheesecloth bag suspended over a frame. A wide bowl is placed underneath to catch the liquid. Do not squeeze the jelly strainer bag or the liquid and resulting jelly will turn cloudy. You can use the pectin test if necessary, but the recipes in this book give you the required amount of sugar for the fruit used. Add sugar, stir until dissolved then boil rapidly for the required time, following the same method for jams. Skimming off scum is essential here or it will make the jelly cloudy. Before pouring into the clean, warm jars, be sure to allow any bubbles in

the pan to subside. Pour the jelly down the sides of the jars to prevent any bubbles forming.

SAVORY PRESERVES

All the basics of jam making apply when cooking savory preserves as well. Generally, they are cooked until thick and pulpy, not watery, and when tested on a plate will leave a clean trail behind without any runny liquid. Choose firm, ripe, and unblemished vegetables. Always use clean, warm jars and equipment, and refrigerate the preserve after opening.

Savory preserves contain a variety of herbs and spices. It is important to remember that dried herbs and spices do lose their flavor if kept too long and this can affect the final flavor of your preserve. It is best to buy in small, rather than large, quantities.

Testing for flavor while the preserve is hot doesn't always give a true indication of the final flavor. The flavors will only develop fully after a few weeks' storage. For a quick idea of the taste, allow a little to cool on a saucer before trying it. Ideally, before making changes to a recipe and adding new flavors, it is best to make the recipe first exactly as described in the book. Then, after storage, taste the preserve and work out what changes you'd like to make the next time you are cooking it.

CHUTNEYS

Long, slow cooking of both vegetables and fruit, with the addition of sugar, vinegar, and spices so that the flavors and colors are both rich and concentrated, produces a thick, flavorsome pulp known as chutney. The flavor variations seem endless, depending on the fruit and vegetables used and the spices added.

Spices play a large part in chutney making and you can change a plain chutney into a deliciously spicy, aromatic one with the addition of chilies, cardamom, and cinnamon, to name just a few. Just be careful not to add too many or you will overpower the flavors of the fruit in the chutney. Chutneys are cooked until very thick. They must be stirred often to prevent sticking and burning on the bottom of the pan. When tested on a plate, they should leave a clean trail behind without any runny liquid.

PICKLES

Preparing vegetables for pickling involves soaking them in a brine (salt and water solution) or layering them sprinkled with salt for 24 hours. The salt draws out moisture from the vegetables, which softens them and removes any excess liquid that may dilute the vinegar. It also adds to the final flavor. The vegetables should be rinsed well under cold running water after salting. They can

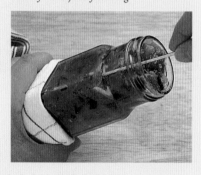

Use a clean, thin metal skewer to remove any air bubbles from the jars before sealing.

Curds are made of fruit, egg, and butter and reach a thick, creamy consistency.

When tested, the chutney should leave a clean trail without any runny liquid.

STORAGE

JAMS, CONSERVES, PRESERVES—Store in an airtight jar in a cool, dark place for 6–12 months. Once opened, store in the refrigerator for 6 weeks.

JELLIES—Store in an airtight jar in a cool, dark place for 6–12 months. Once opened, store in refrigerator for 1 month.

CURDS—Store in an airtight jar in the refrigerator for up to 2 weeks.

FRUIT PASTES—Set in disposable foil trays or wrap in parchment paper, then plastic wrap, then foil and then plastic wrap again. Store in a cool, dark place for 6–12 months.

SAUCES, CHUTNEYS, RELISHES, AND PICKLES—Sauces, chutneys, relishes, and pickles should be left for 1 month before eating to allow the flavors to develop. Store in a cool, dark place for up to 1 year. Once opened, store refrigerated for 6 weeks.

HEAT-PROCESSED FRUITS AND VEGETABLES—Store in a cool, dark place for up to 1 year. Once opened, store in the refrigerator for 1 week.

MUSTARDS—Store in a cool, dark place for up to 3 months. Once jars are opened, refrigerate only for 1–2 weeks.

be left raw or lightly cooked and are packed into clean jars and topped with a vinegar solution. Spices can also be added to increase the flavor.

RELISHES

The method for making relishes is very similar to that for making pickles. First salt the vegetables, then rinse them well under cold, running water. The vegetable mixture is then simmered in a spicy vinegar solution before being thickened with cornstarch or a slurry—a thin paste made from all-purpose flour and water.

CURDS

Gently cooked over a pan of simmering water, curds still require that the basics of jam making are followed. The egg and butter thicken the fruit mixture during cooking and once refrigerated.

FRUIT PASTES

Fruit pastes are a cross between jelly and jam. It is a strained fruit purée, cooked with sugar until thick and pastelike. Again, the basics of jam making apply here, and great care is needed to avoid being splattered with the thick mixture as it bubbles like hot lava in the base of the pan. Take care not to overcook the mixture or let it catch and burn on the bottom. Fruit pastes use a large amount of fruit, so it is best to make them when there is an overabundance available at a reasonable price.

Lemon seeds and peel are often added to the cooking mixture in a small cheesecloth bag.

SWEET JAMS AND PRESERVES

Strawberry jam

INGREDIENTS

10 cups (3 pounds) medium strawberries

½ cup lemon juice

5½ cups sugar, warmed

Put two small plates in the freezer for testing purposes (you may not need the second plate). Wipe the strawberries clean, then remove the stalks and place the strawberries in a large pan with lemon juice, warmed sugar, and ½ cup water. Warm gently, without boiling, stirring gently with a wooden spoon, trying not to break up the strawberries too much.

Increase the heat and, without boiling, stir the mixture for 10 minutes, or until all the sugar has dissolved. Increase the heat and boil for 20 minutes, stirring often. Skim any scum off the surface with a skimmer or slotted spoon. Start testing for setting point after 20 minutes, but it may take up to 40 minutes for the jam to be ready. Be careful that the jam does not catch on the base of the pan and start to burn.

Remove from the heat, place a little jam on one of the cold plates, then place in the freezer for 30 seconds. When setting point is reached, a skin will form on the surface and the jam will wrinkle when pushed with your finger. Remove any scum from the surface.

Spoon immediately into clean, warm jars then seal. Turn the jars upside down for 2 minutes, then invert and let cool. Label and date. Store in a cool, dark place for 6–12 months. Refrigerate after opening for up to 6 weeks.

note WASH STRAWBERRIES BEFORE THEIR STALKS HAVE BEEN REMOVED OR THEY WILL ABSORB WATER AND THEIR TASTE AND TEXTURE WILL BE AFFECTED.

preparation 15 minutes ✳ cooking 1 hour

SWEET JAMS AND PRESERVES

Jelly roll *with strawberry jam*

Here is a cake that looks impressive but is easy to prepare. Just be sure to roll up the cake slowly and carefully. For a treat, spread a layer of whipped cream over the jam.

INGREDIENTS

¾ cup self-rising flour

3 eggs, lightly beaten

¾ cup superfine sugar

½ cup strawberry jam (recipe on previous page),
    beaten

confectioners' sugar, to sprinkle

Preheat the oven to 375°F. Lightly grease a shallow ¾ x 10 x 12-inch jelly roll pan and line the base with parchment paper, extending over the two long sides. Sift the flour three times onto parchment paper.

Beat the eggs using handheld beaters in a small bowl for 5 minutes, or until thick and pale. Add ½ cup of the sugar gradually, beating constantly until the mixture is pale and glossy. Transfer to a large bowl. Using a metal spoon, fold in the flour quickly and lightly. Spread into the pan and smooth the surface. Bake for 10–12 minutes, or until lightly golden and springy to touch. Meanwhile, place a clean dish towel on a work surface, cover with parchment paper and lightly sprinkle with the remaining superfine sugar. When the cake is cooked, turn it out immediately onto the sugar.

Using the dish towel as a guide, carefully roll the cake up from the short side, rolling the paper inside the roll. Stand the rolled cake on a wire rack for 5 minutes, then carefully unroll and allow the cake to cool to room temperature. Spread with the jam and re-roll. Neaten the ends by trimming with a knife. Sprinkle with confectioners' sugar.

preparation 25 minutes ✳ cooking 12 minutes ✳ serves 10

Fig preserve

INGREDIENTS

about 20 (2¼ pounds) medium fresh figs,
    stalks removed

½ cup lemon juice

4⅓ cups sugar, warmed

Put two small plates in the freezer for testing purposes (you may not need the second plate). Put the figs in a large heatproof bowl. Cover with boiling water for 3 minutes. Drain, cool, and cut into pieces.

Place the figs, lemon juice, and ½ cup water in a large pan. Bring to a boil, then reduce the heat and simmer, covered, for 20 minutes, or until the figs are soft. Add the sugar and stir over medium heat, without boiling, for 5 minutes, or until all the sugar has dissolved.

Bring to a boil and boil for 20 minutes, stirring often. Remove any scum from the surface during cooking with a skimmer or a slotted spoon. Add a little water if the mixture thickens too much. When it is thick and pulpy, start testing for setting point.

Remove from the heat, place a little preserve on one of the cold plates, then place in the freezer for 30 seconds. When setting point is reached, a skin will form on the surface and the preserve will wrinkle when pushed with your finger. Remove any scum from the surface.

Pour immediately into clean, warm jars, and seal. Turn the jars upside down for 2 minutes, then invert and let cool. Label and date. Store in a cool, dark place for 6–12 months. Refrigerate preserve after opening for up to 6 weeks.

preparation 20 minutes ✦ cooking 45 minutes

SWEET JAMS AND PRESERVES

Fig and raspberry cake *with fig preserve*

This shortcake is best eaten on the day it is made. The slightly earthy taste of the figs and the intense flavor of fresh raspberries and citrus meld beautifully in this dessert.

INGREDIENTS
¾ cup unsalted butter
¾ cup superfine sugar
1 egg
1 egg yolk
2⅔ cups all-purpose flour
1 teaspoon baking powder
4 medium figs, quartered
shredded zest of 1 medium orange
1⅔ cups raspberries

2 tablespoons sugar, extra
fig preserve (recipe on previous page)
whipped cream or mascarpone, to serve

Preheat the oven to 350°F. Grease a 9-inch springform cake pan.

Cream the butter and sugar in a bowl until light and pale. Add the egg and egg yolk and beat again. Sift the flour and baking powder into the bowl and add a pinch of salt. Stir to combine. Chill for 15 minutes, or until firm enough to roll out.

Divide the dough in two equal halves and roll out one half large enough to fit the base of the pan. Cover with the figs, orange zest, and raspberries. Roll out the remaining dough and place it over the filling. Lightly brush the top with water and sprinkle with the extra sugar. Bake for 30 minutes, or until a skewer inserted into the center of the cake comes out clean. Cut into slices. Stir a little fig preserve gently through whipped cream or mascarpone and serve on the side.

preparation 25 minutes ✦ cooking 30 minutes

THE FRUIT OF LEGEND

One of the most sensual of fruits, with

their velvety skins and seed-filled flesh,

figs held mythological status in ancient Rome

and Greece where they were not only a chief

source of sustenance for the original Olympians,

but so important to the Greek diet that

it became illegal to export them.

Mixed berry jam

INGREDIENTS

about 7 cups (2¼ pounds) mixed berries
(strawberries, raspberries, blackberries,
blueberries, mulberries)

⅓ cup lemon juice

4⅓ cups sugar, warmed

1 tablespoon and 2 teaspoons (1 ounce)
jam-setting mixture

Place the berries and lemon juice in a large pan and gently cook for 10 minutes. Add the sugar and stir over low heat for 5 minutes, or until all the sugar has dissolved.

Boil for 15 minutes, stirring often, and then remove from the heat. Add the jam setting mixture, then return the berry mixture to the heat and boil rapidly for a further 5 minutes. Remove any scum from the surface with a skimmer or slotted spoon.

Pour immediately into clean, warm jars, and seal. Turn the jars upside down for 2 minutes, then invert and let cool. Label and date. Store the jars in a cool, dark place for 6–12 months. Refrigerate after opening for up to 6 weeks.

note REMOVE THE STEMS, STALKS, LEAVES, AND ANY BLEMISHES FROM THE BERRIES YOU HAVE CHOSEN. IF THE BERRIES ARE SANDY OR GRITTY, WASH THEM GENTLY UNDER COLD WATER AND DRAIN WELL IN A COLANDER TO REMOVE AS MUCH WATER AS POSSIBLE BEFORE USE. USE A MIXTURE OF FRESH AND FROZEN BERRIES, IF NECESSARY.

preparation 20 minutes ✦ cooking 35 minutes

BISCUITS

2½ cups self-rising flour

1 teaspoon baking powder

2 tablespoons chilled unsalted butter cut into small cubes

1 cup milk

Preheat the oven to 425°F. Lightly grease a cookie tray or line with parchment paper. Sift the flour, baking powder, and a pinch of salt into a bowl. Using your fingertips, rub in the butter briefly and lightly until the mixture resembles fine bread crumbs. Mix in the sugar. Make a well in the center. Pour in almost all of the milk and mix with a flat-bladed knife, using a cutting action until the dough comes together in clumps. Rotate the bowl as you work. Use the remaining milk if the mixture seems dry. Handle the mixture with great care and a very light hand. The dough should feel slightly wet and sticky. With floured hands, gently gather the dough together, lift onto a lightly floured surface, then pat into a smooth ball. Do not knead or the biscuits will be tough.

Pat or lightly roll the dough out to ¾-inch thick. Using a floured 2½-inch cutter, cut into rounds. Don't pat out too thinly or the biscuits will not be a good height. Gather the scraps together and, without overhandling them, press out as before and cut out more rounds. Place close together on the cookie tray and lightly brush the tops with milk.

Bake in the top half of the oven for 12–15 minutes, or until risen and golden. If you aren't sure if they are cooked, break one open. If still doughy in the center, cook for a few more minutes. For soft biscuits, wrap in a dry dish towel while hot. For biscuits with a crisp top, transfer to a wire rack to cool slightly before wrapping. Serve warm with jam and whipped cream.

PREPARATION 20 MINUTES
COOKING 12–15 MINUTES
MAKES 10–12

Apricot and passion fruit jam

INGREDIENTS

about 20 (2⅓ pounds) medium fresh apricots, pits removed

4⅓ cups sugar, warmed

⅔ cup passion fruit pulp

2 tablespoons lemon juice

Put two small plates in the freezer for testing purposes (you may not need the second plate). Cut the apricots into quarters and place in a large pan with ⅓ cup water. Cover and cook over low heat for 10 minutes, or until tender.

Remove from the heat and add the sugar, passion fruit pulp, and lemon juice. Heat slowly, stirring, for about 5 minutes, or until all the sugar has dissolved. Return to a boil and boil rapidly for 30 minutes, stirring often. Remove any scum during cooking with a skimmer or slotted spoon. When the jam falls from a tilted wooden spoon in thick sheets without dripping, start testing for setting point.

Remove from the heat, place a little jam on one of the cold plates, then place in the freezer for 30 seconds. When setting point is reached, a skin will form on the surface and the jam will wrinkle when pushed with your finger. Remove any scum from the surface.

Spoon immediately into clean, warm jars and seal. Turn the jars upside down for 2 minutes, then invert and let cool. Label and date. Store in a cool, dark place for 6–12 months. Refrigerate after opening for up to 6 weeks.

preparation 15 minutes ✳ cooking 45 minutes

Raspberry jam

INGREDIENTS

about 12 cups (3 pounds) fresh or
  frozen raspberries

⅓ cup lemon juice

6½ cups sugar, warmed

Put two small plates in the freezer for testing purposes (you may not need the second plate). Place the berries and lemon juice in a large pan. Stir over low heat for 10 minutes, or until the berries are soft.

Add the sugar and stir, without boiling, for 5 minutes, or until all the sugar has dissolved.

Bring the mixture to a boil and boil for 20 minutes. Stir often and make sure the jam doesn't stick or burn on the base of the pan. Remove any scum during cooking with a skimmer or slotted spoon. When the jam falls from a tilted wooden spoon in thick sheets without dripping, start testing for setting point.

Remove from the heat, place a little jam on one of the cold plates, then place in the freezer for 30 seconds. When setting point is reached, a skin will form on the surface and the jam will wrinkle when pushed with your finger. Remove any scum.

Spoon immediately into clean, warm jars and seal. Turn the jars upside down for 2 minutes, then invert and let cool. Label and date. Store in a cool, dark place for 6–12 months. Refrigerate after opening for up to 6 weeks.

note FROZEN RASPBERRIES CAN BE USED, BUT THE COOKING TIME SHOULD BE INCREASED BY A FEW MINUTES.

preparation 10 minutes ✦ cooking 35 minutes

Princess fingers *with raspberry jam*

Bars are the perfect thing to make to go with coffee. This attractive one is packed with nuts, jam, and coconut and can be made a couple of days in advance.

INGREDIENTS

½ cup unsalted butter, cubed and softened

⅓ cup superfine sugar

1 teaspoon vanilla extract

2 egg yolks

2 cups all-purpose flour

1 teaspoon baking powder

1 tablespoon milk

½ cup raspberry jam (recipe on previous page)

⅓ cup chopped walnuts

⅓ cup chopped red candied cherries

2 egg whites

1 tablespoon shredded orange zest

½ cup superfine sugar, extra

½ cup shredded coconut

1 cup puffed rice cereal

Preheat the oven to 350°F. Lightly grease a 8 x 12-inch jelly roll pan and line with parchment paper, leaving the paper hanging over on the two long sides. Cream the butter, sugar, and vanilla using handheld beaters until light and fluffy. Add the egg yolks, one at a time, beating well after each addition.

Sift the flour and baking powder into a bowl, then fold into the creamed mixture with a metal spoon. Fold in the milk, then press evenly and firmly into the pan. Spread the jam over the surface and sprinkle with the chopped walnuts and cherries.

Beat the egg whites in a small, dry bowl until stiff peaks form. Fold in the orange zest and extra sugar with a metal spoon, then fold in the coconut and puffed rice cereal. Spread over the bar with a metal spatula.

Bake for 30–35 minutes, or until firm and golden brown. Cool the bar in the pan. Lift out the bar, using the paper as handles, and cut into fingers. This bar can be kept for up to 4 days in an airtight container.

preparation 35 minutes ✳ cooking 35 minutes ✳ makes 24 pieces

Blueberry preserve

INGREDIENTS
about 6 cups (2¼ pounds) blueberries
¼ cup lemon juice (and the seeds of 1 medium lemon)
4⅓ cups sugar, warmed

Put two small plates in the freezer for testing purposes (you may not need the second plate). Place the berries in a large pan with ¾ cup water. Place the lemon seeds on a piece of cheesecloth and tie securely with string. Add the cheesecloth bag to the pan. Cook over low heat for 5 minutes, or until the berries just start to color the water.

Add the lemon juice and sugar, and stir over low heat for 5 minutes, or until all the sugar has dissolved. Bring slowly to a boil and cook for 20–25 minutes, stirring often. Remove any scum during cooking with a skimmer or slotted spoon. When the preserve falls from a tilted wooden spoon in thick sheets without dripping, start testing for setting point.

Remove from the heat, place a little preserve on one of the cold plates. Place in the freezer for 30 seconds. When setting point is reached, a skin will form on the surface and the preserve will wrinkle when pushed with your finger. Remove any scum from the surface.

Transfer to a heatproof pitcher and pour immediately into clean, warm jars and seal. Turn the jars upside down for 2 minutes, then invert and let cool. Label and date. Store in a cool, dark place for 6–12 months. Refrigerate after opening for up to 6 weeks.

preparation 10 minutes ✳ cooking 35 minutes

SWEET JAMS AND PRESERVES

Peach conserve

INGREDIENTS
about 9 (3⅓ pounds) large peaches
1 medium green apple
1 medium lemon
4⅓ cups sugar, warmed

Put two small plates in the freezer for testing purposes (you may not need the second plate). Score a cross in the base of each peach. Place the peaches in a large heatproof bowl and cover with boiling water. Leave for 1–2 minutes, then remove with a slotted spoon. Cool slightly and peel. Halve, then remove the pit and chop the flesh into 1-inch pieces.

Chop the apple, including the peel and core, into ½-inch pieces. Peel thin strips of peel from the lemon, then cut it in half and juice. Place the apple and lemon peel onto a square of cheesecloth and tie securely with string.

Place the chopped peaches, cheesecloth bag, and 1¼ cups water in a large pan. Bring slowly to a boil, then reduce the heat and simmer for 30 minutes, or until the peaches are tender. Remove any scum from the surface during cooking with a skimmer or slotted spoon. Squeeze any excess juice from the cheesecloth bag by pushing firmly against the side of the pan, then discard the bag.

Add the sugar and stir over low heat for 5 minutes, or until all the sugar has dissolved. Add the lemon juice, return to a boil and boil rapidly for 30 minutes, stirring often. Stir across the base of the pan to check that the conserve is not sticking or burning. When the conserve falls from a tilted wooden spoon in thick sheets without dripping, start testing for setting point.

Remove from heat, place a little conserve on one of the cold plates, then place in the freezer for 30 seconds. When setting point is reached, a skin will form on the surface and the conserve will wrinkle when pushed with your finger. Remove any scum from the surface.

Spoon immediately into clean, warm jars and seal. Turn the jars upside down for 2 minutes, then invert and let cool. Label and date. Store in a cool, dark place for 6–12 months. Refrigerate after opening for up to 6 weeks.

preparation 20 minutes ＊ cooking 1 hour 5 minutes

Tomato and pineapple jam

INGREDIENTS
about 13 (4½ pounds) medium ripe tomatoes
6½ cups sugar, warmed
½ cup lemon juice
2¾ cups canned crushed pineapple, drained

Put two small plates in the freezer for testing purposes (you may not need the second plate). Cut a cross in the base of each tomato. Place tomatoes in a large bowl, cover with boiling water and leave for 30 seconds, or until the skins start to spilt. Transfer tomatoes to a bowl of cold water. Remove skin and chop the flesh.

Place the tomato in a large pan. Add half the warmed sugar and simmer for 5–10 minutes over low heat, stirring, until the tomato has softened and all the sugar has dissolved.

Add the lemon juice, pineapple, and remaining sugar. Stir over low heat until all the sugar has dissolved. Bring to a boil and cook for 30–35 minutes, stirring frequently. Remove any scum from the surface during cooking with a skimmer or slotted spoon. When the jam falls from a tilted wooden spoon in thick sheets without dripping, start testing for setting point.

Remove from the heat, place a little jam on one of the cold plates, then place in the freezer for 30 seconds. When setting point is reached, a skin will form on the surface and the jam will wrinkle when pushed with your finger. Remove any scum from the surface.

Spoon immediately into clean, warm jars and seal. Turn the jars upside down for 2 minutes, then invert and let cool. Label and date. Store in a cool, dark place for 6–12 months. Refrigerate after opening for up to 6 weeks.

note CHOOSE TOMATOES THAT ARE VERY RIPE TO MAXIMIZE THE TASTE OF YOUR JAM. VINE-RIPENED TOMATOES, WHILE EXPENSIVE, GENERALLY HAVE THE BEST FLAVOR.

preparation 20 minutes ✦ cooking 35 minutes

SWEET JAMS AND PRESERVES

Blood plum jam

INGREDIENTS
25 (4½ pounds) medium blood plums
½ cup lemon juice
6½ cups sugar, warmed

Put two small plates in the freezer for testing purposes (you may not need the second plate). Cut the plums in half and remove the pits. Crack a few pits and remove the kernels. Place the kernels in a piece of cheesecloth and tie securely with string. Place the plums and the bag in a large pan and add 4 cups water. Bring slowly to a boil, reduce the heat and simmer, covered, for 50 minutes, or until the fruit has softened.

Add the lemon juice and sugar and stir over low heat, without boiling, for 5 minutes, or until all the sugar has dissolved. Bring to a boil and boil for 20 minutes, stirring often. Remove any scum from the surface during cooking with a skimmer or slotted spoon. When the jam falls from a tilted wooden spoon in thick sheets without dripping, start testing for setting point.

Remove from the heat, place a little jam on one of the cold plates, then place in the freezer for 30 seconds. When setting point is reached, a skin will form on the surface and the jam will wrinkle when pushed with your finger. Remove any scum from the surface.

Spoon immediately into clean, warm jars and seal. Turn the jars upside down for 2 minutes, then invert and let cool. Label and date. Store in a cool, dark place for 6–12 months. Refrigerate after opening for up to 6 weeks.

note BLOOD PLUMS HAVE DARK SKIN AND DARK FLESH. IF UNAVAILABLE, ANY KIND OF PLUM CAN BE USED.

preparation 20 minutes ✴ cooking 1 hour 15 minutes

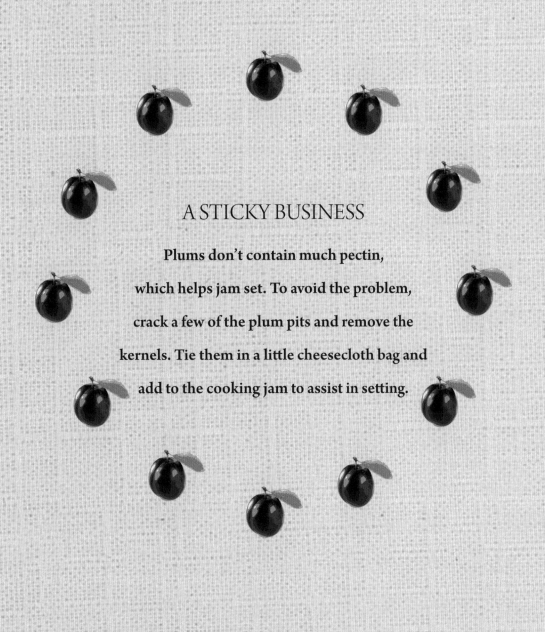

A STICKY BUSINESS

Plums don't contain much pectin,
which helps jam set. To avoid the problem,
crack a few of the plum pits and remove the
kernels. Tie them in a little cheesecloth bag and
add to the cooking jam to assist in setting.

Monte creams *with blood plum jam*

It is said that this favorite takes its name from the glamorous city of Monte Carlo. Whatever the reason, it's a delicious cookie.

INGREDIENTS
½ cup unsalted butter
½ cup superfine sugar
¼ cup milk
1½ cups self-rising flour
¼ cup instant vanilla pudding mix
⅓ cup shredded coconut
instant vanilla pudding mix, extra

FILLING
heaping ¼ cup unsalted butter, softened
⅔ cup confectioners' sugar
2 teaspoons milk
⅓ cup blood plum jam (recipe on page 39)

Preheat the oven to 350°F. Line two cookie trays with parchment paper. Cream the butter and sugar in a small bowl using handheld beaters until light and fluffy. Add the milk and beat until combined. Sift the flour and pudding mix and add to the bowl with the coconut. Mix to form a soft dough.

Roll 2 teaspoons of the mixture into balls. Place on the trays and press with a fork. Dip the fork in the extra pudding mix occasionally to prevent it from sticking. Bake for 15–20 minutes, or until just golden. Transfer to a wire rack to cool completely before filling.

To make the filling, beat the butter and confectioners' sugar in a small bowl using handheld beaters until light and creamy. Beat in the milk. Spread one cookie with ½ teaspoon of the filling and one with ½ teaspoon of jam, then press them together.

preparation 30 minutes ✦ cooking 20 minutes ✦ makes 25

Rhubarb and ginger jam

INGREDIENTS

12 cups (3 pounds 5 ounces) chopped rhubarb

6¾ cups sugar, warmed

½ cup lemon juice

1½-inch piece fresh ginger, bruised and halved

½ cup candied ginger, finely chopped

Layer the rhubarb, sugar, and lemon juice in a large nonmetallic bowl. Cover and leave overnight.

Put two small plates in the freezer for testing purposes (you may not need the second plate). Place the rhubarb mixture in a large pan. Finely chop the fresh ginger and place on a square of cheesecloth. Tie securely with string and add to the pan. Stir over a low heat for 5 minutes, or until all the sugar has dissolved. Bring to a boil and boil rapidly for 20–30 minutes, stirring often. Remove any scum during cooking with a skimmer or slotted spoon. When the jam falls from a tilted wooden spoon in thick sheets without dripping, start testing for setting point.

Remove from the heat, place a little jam on one of the cold plates, then place in the freezer for 30 seconds. When setting point is reached, a skin will form on the surface and the jam will wrinkle when pushed with your finger. Remove any scum and discard the cheesecloth bag. Add the candied ginger to the pan.

Spoon immediately into clean, warm jars, and seal. Turn the jars upside down for 2 minutes, then invert and let cool. Label and date. Store in a cool, dark place for 6–12 months. Refrigerate after opening for up to 6 weeks.

note THE AMOUNT OF GINGER CAN BE VARIED, ACCORDING TO TASTE.

preparation 15 minutes + overnight soaking ✳ cooking 35 minutes

SWEET JAMS AND PRESERVES

Apricot jam

INGREDIENTS
about 15 (2¼ pounds) medium apricots,
   pits removed, quartered
4⅓ cups sugar, warmed

Put two small plates in the freezer for testing purposes (you may not need the second plate).

Put the apricots in a large pan with 1½ cups water. Bring to a boil, stirring, for 20 minutes, or until the fruit has softened.

Add the sugar and stir, without boiling, for 5 minutes, or until all the sugar has dissolved. Return to a boil and boil for 20 minutes, stirring often. Stir across the base of the pan to check that the jam is not sticking or burning. Remove any scum during cooking with a skimmer or slotted spoon. When the jam falls from a tilted wooden spoon in thick sheets without dripping, start testing for setting point.

Remove from the heat, place a little jam on one of the cold plates, then place in the freezer for 30 seconds. When setting point is reached, a skin will form on the surface and the jam will wrinkle when pushed with your finger. Remove any scum.

Spoon immediately into clean, warm jars and seal. Turn the jars upside down for 2 minutes, then invert and let cool. Label and date. Store in a cool, dark place for 6–12 months. Refrigerate after opening for up to 6 weeks.

preparation 20 minutes ✦ cooking 45 minutes

Frozen berry jam

INGREDIENTS
2¼ cups (10 ounces) frozen blackberries
2¼ cups (10 ounces) frozen raspberries
2¼ cups (10 ounces) frozen blueberries
¼ cup lemon juice, reserving any seeds
3 cups sugar, warmed

Put two small plates in the freezer for testing purposes (you may not need the second plate). Put the frozen berries in a large pan with 3 cups water and the lemon juice.

Place the seeds on a square of cheesecloth and tie securely with string. Add to the pan. Bring to a boil, then reduce the heat and simmer for 30 minutes.

Add the sugar and stir over low heat for 5 minutes, or until all the sugar has dissolved. Return to a boil and boil for 30–40 minutes, stirring often. Remove any scum during cooking with a skimmer or slotted spoon. When the jam falls from a tilted wooden spoon in thick sheets without dripping, start testing for setting point.

Remove from the heat, place a little jam on one of the cold plates, then place in the freezer for 30 seconds. A skin will form on the surface and the jam will wrinkle when pushed with your finger when setting point is reached. Discard the cheesecloth bag. Remove any scum from the surface.

Spoon immediately into clean, warm jars and seal. Turn the jars upside down for 2 minutes, then invert and let cool. Label and date. Store in a cool, dark place for 6–12 months. Refrigerate after opening for up to 6 weeks.

preparation 10 minutes * cooking 1 hour 15 minutes

SWEET JAMS AND PRESERVES

Banana jam

INGREDIENTS

about 7 (2¼ pounds) very ripe bananas, peeled (see Note)

5 tablespoons lemon juice

3 cups sugar, warmed

Chop the bananas and place in a large pan with the lemon juice and sugar. Bring to a boil and skim any scum with a skimmer or slotted spoon.

Cook the jam over medium heat for 30 minutes, then reduce the heat and simmer, stirring frequently, for 15–20 minutes, or until the jam is thick and pale red in color. Remove any scum from the surface.

Spoon immediately into clean, warm jars, and seal. Turn the jars upside down for 2 minutes, then invert and let cool. Label and date. Store in a cool, dark place for 6–12 months. Refrigerate after opening for up to 6 weeks.

notes USE VERY MUSHY BANANAS, SIMILAR TO THOSE YOU WOULD USE FOR A BANANA CAKE. WHILE NOT A TRUE JAM, THIS IS JUST AS DELICIOUS. SERVE AS YOU WOULD OTHER FRUIT JAMS.

preparation 10 minutes ✦ cooking 50 minutes

Banana muffins *with banana jam*

Every lunch box deserves a good muffin, and this recipe delivers. Moist and light, they are even better served with coffee and spread with a generous amount of banana jam.

INGREDIENTS

2½ cups self-rising flour

¾ cup superfine sugar

½ teaspoon pumpkin pie spice

1 cup milk

2 eggs, lightly beaten

1 teaspoon vanilla extract

heaping ½ cup unsalted butter, melted and cooled

1 cup mashed ripe banana

banana jam, for spreading (recipe on previous page)

Preheat the oven to 400°F. Lightly grease a 12-hole standard muffin pan, or line the muffin pan with paper liners. Sift the flour into a bowl. Add the sugar and pumpkin pie spice to the bowl and stir through the flour. Make a well in the center.

Mix together the milk, eggs, and vanilla. Pour the liquid into the well in the flour and add the cooled butter and banana. Fold the mixture gently with a metal spoon until just combined. Do not overmix; the batter will still be slightly lumpy. Divide the mixture evenly among the holes, filling each hole to about three-quarters full.

Bake the muffins for 20–25 minutes, or until they are golden and a skewer inserted in the center of a muffin comes out clean. Leave the muffins in the pan for a couple of minutes to cool. Gently loosen each muffin with a flat-bladed knife before turning out onto a wire rack. Serve warm or at room temperature, spread with banana jam.

preparation 20 minutes ✳ cooking 25 minutes ✳ makes 12

MINCEMEAT BAR

2 cups all-purpose flour
½ cup confectioners' sugar
¾ cup unsalted butter, cubed
1 egg
1¼ cups mincemeat
⅔ cup pitted prunes, chopped
½ cup candied ginger, chopped
1 egg, lightly beaten
confectioners' sugar, extra, to dust

Preheat the oven to 375°F. Lightly grease a shallow 7 x 11¼-inch pan and line the base with parchment paper, leaving the paper hanging over the two long sides. Sift the flour and confectioners' sugar into a large bowl. Rub in the butter with your fingertips until the mixture resembles fine bread crumbs. Make a well in the center and add the egg. Mix with a flat-bladed knife, using a cutting action, until the mixture comes together. Turn onto a lightly floured surface and press together until smooth.

Divide the dough in half and press one portion into the pan. Bake for 10 minutes, then let cool. Roll the remaining pastry out on a piece of parchment paper; refrigerate for 15 minutes. Spread the mincemeat evenly over the baked pastry, topping it with the prunes and ginger. Cut the rolled pastry into thin strips with a sharp knife or fluted pastry wheel. Arrange on top of the fruit in a diagonal lattice pattern. Brush with the beaten egg. Bake for 30 minutes, or until golden. Cool in the pan, then lift out, using the paper as handles, and cut into squares or fingers. Serve dusted with confectioners' sugar. The bar can be kept for up to 4 days if stored in an airtight container in a cool place, or in the refrigerator.

PREPARATION 20 MINUTES
COOKING 40 MINUTES
MAKES 15

Traditional mincemeat

INGREDIENTS
2 large green apples, peeled, cored, and
   finely chopped
8 ounces suet
1½ cups firmly packed light brown sugar
3 cups raisins
2 cups golden raisins
2 cups currants
¾ cup candied peel
¾ cup slivered almonds, chopped
1 tablespoon pumpkin pie spice
½ teaspoon ground nutmeg
½ teaspoon cinnamon
2 teaspoons shredded orange peel
1 teaspoon shredded lemon peel
1 cup orange juice
½ cup lemon juice
5 fluid ounces brandy

Combine all the ingredients and ½ cup of the brandy in a large bowl. Combine thoroughly.

Spoon the mincemeat into clean, warm jars. Use a skewer to remove air bubbles and to pack the mixture in firmly. Leave a ½-inch space at the top of the jar and wipe the jar clean with a cloth. Spoon remaining brandy over the surface of the mincemeat and seal. Label and date.

Set aside for at least 3 weeks, or up to 6 months, before using in pies and tarts. Keep the mincemeat refrigerated in hot weather.

preparation 20 minutes ✴ no cooking required

SWEET JAMS AND PRESERVES

Mincemeat pies *using traditional mincemeat*

A warm mincemeat pie on a cold winter's day is a very comforting thing. And, mincemeat pies are, of course, synonymous with holiday fare.

INGREDIENTS
PASTRY
2 cups all-purpose flour
⅔ cup chilled unsalted butter, cubed
⅔ cup confectioners' sugar

2–3 tablespoons iced water
confectioners' sugar, extra, to dust
traditional mincemeat (recipe on previous page)

Preheat the oven to 350°F. Lightly grease two 12-hole mini muffin pans.

To make the pastry, sift the flour into a bowl. Using your fingertips, rub in the butter until the mixture resembles fine bread crumbs. Stir in the confectioners' sugar and make a well in the center. Add almost all the water and mix with a flat-bladed knife, using a cutting action, until the mixture comes together in beads. Add the remaining water if the dough is too dry. Turn out onto a lightly floured work surface and gather into a ball. Roll out two-thirds of the pastry and cut out 24 rounds, slightly larger than the holes in the muffin pans, with a round fluted cutter. Fit the rounds into the pans.

Divide the mincemeat evenly among the pastry cases. Roll out the remaining pastry, a little thinner than before, and cut 12 rounds with the same cutter. Using a smaller fluted cutter, cut 12 more rounds. Place the large circles on top of half the pies and press the edges to seal. Place the smaller circles on the remainder. Bake for 25 minutes, or until golden. Leave in the pans for 5 minutes, then lift out with a knife and cool on wire racks. Dust lightly with confectioners' sugar. Eat within a couple of days.

preparation 30 minutes + cooking 25 minutes + makes 24

Pineapple and mango jam

INGREDIENTS

1 medium pineapple (choose a ripe one)

2 large mangoes

1 teaspoon lemon peel, shredded

⅓ cup lemon juice, reserving the seeds and skin of 1 lemon

5 cups warmed sugar

Put two small plates in the freezer for testing purposes (you may not need the second plate). Remove the skin and tough eyes from the pineapple. Cut the pineapple into quarters lengthways, then remove the core and cut the flesh into ½- inch pieces. Peel the mango and cut each mango cheek from the pit. Cut into ½-inch pieces. Place the pineapple, mango, any juices, lemon peel and juice, and sugar in a large pan and stir for 5 minutes, or until all the sugar has dissolved.

Place the reserved seeds and skin of the lemon on a square of cheesecloth, then tie securely with string and add to the pan.

Bring to a boil, then reduce the heat and simmer, stirring often, for 30–40 minutes, or until setting point is reached. Remove any scum during cooking with a skimmer or slotted spoon. Stir across the base of the pan to check that the jam is not sticking or burning. Be careful because the jam will froth. When the jam falls from a tilted wooden spoon in thick sheets without dripping, start testing for setting point.

Remove from the heat, place a little jam on one of the cold plates, then place in the freezer for 30 seconds. A skin will form on the surface and the jam will wrinkle when pushed with your finger when setting point is reached. Remove any scum from the surface.

Pour immediately into clean, warm jars and seal. Turn upside down for 2 minutes, then invert and cool. Label and date. Store in a cool, dark place for 6–12 months. Refrigerate after opening for up to 6 weeks.

preparation 30 minutes ✴ cooking 45 minutes

Blackberry and apple jam

INGREDIENTS
4 medium green apples
7½ cups (2 pounds) blackberries
6½ cups sugar, warmed

Put two small plates in the freezer for testing purposes (you may not need the second plate). Peel, core and then chop the apples. Place the apple pieces in a large pan with the berries and ½ cup water. Cook, covered, over medium heat, stirring often, for 30 minutes, or until the fruit has softened.

Add the sugar and stir, without boiling, for 5 minutes, or until all the sugar has dissolved.

Bring the jam to a boil and boil for 20 minutes, stirring often. Stir across the base of the pan to check that the jam is not sticking or burning. When the jam falls from a tilted wooden spoon in thick sheets without dripping, start testing for setting point.

Remove from the heat, place a little jam onto one of the cold plates, then place in the freezer for 30 seconds. A skin will form on the surface and the jam will wrinkle when pushed with your finger when setting point is reached. Remove any scum from the surface with a skimmer or slotted spoon.

Transfer to a heatproof pitcher and immediately pour into clean, warm jars, and seal. Turn upside down for 2 minutes, then invert and let cool. Label and date. Store in a cool, dark place for 6–12 months. Refrigerate after opening for up to 6 weeks.

preparation 20 minutes ✦ cooking 55 minutes

SWEET JAMS AND PRESERVES

Melon and lemon conserve

INGREDIENTS
about 1 medium–large (5½ pounds) honeydew melon
6 lemons
1 tablespoon brandy
5½ cups sugar, warmed

Put two small plates in the freezer for testing purposes (you may not need the second plate). Peel and seed the melons. Cut into ½-inch cubes and add to a large pan.

Scrub the lemons under hot, running water with a soft bristle brush to remove the wax coating, then cut them in half. Juice the lemons, retaining the seeds, and add the juice to the pan. Roughly chop the lemons and divide the pieces and the seeds between two squares of cheesecloth. Tie securely with string and add to the pan along with the brandy and 3 cups water. Bring to a boil and boil for 40 minutes, or until the fruit is soft.

Add the sugar and stir over low heat, without boiling, for 5 minutes, or until all the sugar has dissolved. Bring to a boil and boil, stirring often, for 30 minutes. As the mixture thickens and starts to darken, reduce the heat and simmer, stirring frequently, for 20–30 minutes. When the conserve falls from a tilted wooden spoon in thick sheets without dripping, start testing for setting point.

Remove from the heat, place a little conserve on one cold plate and place in the freezer for 30 seconds. A skin will form on the surface and the conserve will wrinkle when pushed with your finger when setting point is reached. Discard the cheesecloth bags. Remove any scum from the surface.

Spoon immediately into clean, warm jars and seal. Turn the jars upside down for 2 minutes, then invert and let cool. Label and date. Store jars in a cool, dark place for 6–12 months. Refrigerate after opening for up to 6 weeks.

preparation 25 minutes ✦ cooking 1 hour 45 minutes

Black cherry jam

INGREDIENTS

about 3 cups (2¼ pounds) fresh black
    cherries
½ cup lemon juice
3 cups sugar, warmed
1 ounce jam-setting mixture, if required

Put two small plates in the freezer. Remove the stalks from the cherries and, using a small sharp knife, cut the cherries open and remove the seeds. Alternatively, use a cherry pitter, available from kitchenware stores. Place the seeds on a square of cheesecloth and tie securely with string.

Place the cherries and cheesecloth bag in a large pan together with 1 cup water and the lemon juice. Bring to a boil, then reduce the heat and simmer, stirring often, for 30 minutes, or until the cherries are tender. Discard the cheesecloth bag.

Add the sugar and stir over low heat, without boiling, for 5 minutes, or until all the sugar has dissolved. Return the mixture to a boil and boil for 15–20 minutes, stirring often. Remove any scum with a skimmer or slotted spoon.

Remove from the heat, place a little jam on one of the cold plates then place in the freezer for 30 seconds. A skin will form on the surface and the jam will wrinkle when pushed with your finger when setting point is reached. If the jam doesn't set, add the jam-setting mixture, return to the heat and boil rapidly for 5 minutes. Remove any scum from the surface. Spoon immediately into clean, warm jars and seal. Turn the jars upside down for 2 minutes, then invert and let cool. Label and date. Store in a cool, dark place for 6–12 months. Refrigerate after opening for up to 6 weeks.

note CHERRIES ARE LOW IN PECTIN AND JAM-SETTING MIXTURE IS OFTEN ADDED. IF IT IS UNAVAILABLE, BOIL THE JAM FOR A LITTLE LONGER AND ADD MORE LEMON JUICE.

preparation 20 minutes * cooking 1 hour

SWEET JAMS AND PRESERVES

Spiced dried peach conserve

INGREDIENTS

3 dried peaches, each cut into 2 or 3 pieces

2 cinnamon sticks

3 cloves

3 cardamom pods

5½ cups sugar, warmed

¼ cup lemon juice

Place the dried peaches in a nonmetallic bowl, add 7 cups water, cover and soak overnight.

Put two small plates in the freezer for testing purposes (you may not need the second plate). Pour the peaches and water into a large pan. Place the spices on a square of cheesecloth and tie securely with string. Add to the pan with 1 cup water. Bring to a boil, then reduce the heat and simmer for 20 minutes, or until the fruit is soft.

Add the sugar and lemon juice and stir over low heat, without boiling, for 5 minutes, or until all the sugar has dissolved. Return to a boil and boil for 20–25 minutes, stirring often. Remove any scum from the surface during cooking with a skimmer or slotted spoon. When the conserve falls from a tilted wooden spoon in thick sheets without dripping, start testing for setting point.

Remove from heat, place a little conserve on one of the cold plates, then place in the freezer for 30 seconds. A skin will form on the surface and the conserve will wrinkle when pushed with your finger when setting point is reached. Discard the cheesecloth bag. Remove any scum from the surface.

Spoon immediately into clean, warm jars. Turn upside down for 2 minutes, then invert and let cool. Label and date. Store in a cool, dark place for 6–12 months. Refrigerate after opening for up to 6 weeks.

preparation 15 minutes + overnight soaking + cooking 50 minutes

Boysenberry jam

INGREDIENTS
about 7½ cups (2¼ pounds) fresh boysenberries
⅓ cup lemon juice
4⅓ cups sugar, warmed

Put two small plates in the freezer for testing purposes (you may not need the second plate). Put the berries and lemon juice in a large pan and cook gently for 10 minutes. Add the sugar, stir over low heat for 5 minutes, or until all the sugar has dissolved.

Bring to a boil and boil, stirring, for 20 minutes. Remove any scum with a skimmer or slotted spoon during cooking. When the jam falls from a tilted wooden spoon in thick sheets without dripping, start testing for setting point.

Remove from the heat, place a little jam on one of the cold plates, then place in the freezer for 30 seconds. A skin will form on the surface and the jam will wrinkle when pushed with your finger when setting point is reached. Remove any scum from the surface.

Pour immediately into clean, warm jars and seal. Turn the jars upside down for 2 minutes, then invert and let cool. Label and date. Store in a cool, dark place for 6–12 months. Refrigerate after opening for up to 6 weeks.

note IF BOYSENBERRIES ARE NOT AVAILABLE, ANY SOFT BERRY CAN BE USED, SUCH AS MULBERRIES, RASPBERRIES, OR BLACKBERRIES.

preparation 20 minutes * cooking 35 minutes

SWEET JAMS AND PRESERVES

EUROPEAN AND ASIAN PEARS

European pears are classically "pear-shaped"

and have sweet, buttery, slightly "gritty" flesh

that is balanced by an amount of acid.

Varieties include Bosc, Bartlett, and D'anjou.

Asian pears, also called nashi (which simply

means "pear" in Japanese)

are round and have very crisp, juicy,

sweet flesh that is mild in flavor.

Pear and ginger conserve

INGREDIENTS
about 6½ (3 pounds) medium Bosc pears
¼ cup lemon juice
1 teaspoon shredded lemon peel
6½ cups sugar, warmed
⅔ cup candied ginger, finely chopped

Put two small plates in the freezer for testing purposes (you may not need the second plate). Peel, halve then core the pears. Cut the pear flesh into ½-inch pieces. Place the cores and seeds on a piece of cheesecloth, gather up, and tie securely with string. Add to a large pan with the fruit, lemon juice and peel, and 1 cup water.

Bring to a boil, then reduce the heat and simmer for 20–25 minutes, or until the pear is soft. Add sugar and candied ginger and stir over low heat, without boiling, for 5–10 minutes, or until the sugar has dissolved. Return to a boil and boil for 20–25 minutes, stirring often. Remove any scum during cooking with a skimmer or slotted spoon. When the conserve falls from a tilted wooden spoon in thick sheets without dripping, start testing for setting point.

Remove from heat, place a little conserve on one of the cold plates, then place in the freezer for 30 seconds. A skin will form on the surface and the conserve will wrinkle when pushed with your finger when setting point is reached. Discard the cheesecloth bag. Remove any scum from the surface.

Spoon immediately into clean, warm jars. Turn upside down for 2 minutes, then invert and let cool. Label and date. Store in a cool, dark place for 6–12 months. Refrigerate after opening for up to 6 weeks.

preparation 30 minutes ✳ cooking 1 hour

Winter fruit conserve

INGREDIENTS

6½ medium pears (3 pounds), peeled, cored

1 medium grapefruit

1 medium orange

1 medium lemon

6½ cups sugar, warmed

2 cups raisins

½ cup golden raisins

⅓ cup whiskey

Put the pears in a food processor. Scrub the grapefruit, orange, and lemon under warm, running water with a soft bristle brush to remove the wax coating, then halve and thinly slice, removing the seeds. Chop the flesh and add to food processor with any juices. Process in batches until finely chopped and pulpy. Transfer to a large nonmetallic bowl. Stir in the sugar, cover and leave overnight.

Place the mixture in a large pan and bring to a boil. Reduce the heat and simmer for 45 minutes, stirring often. Remove any scum during cooking with a skimmer or slotted spoon.

Add raisins and golden raisins and cook, stirring often, for 45 minutes, or until thick and pulpy. Remove from the heat and stir in the whiskey.

Spoon immediately into clean, warm jars and seal. Turn the jars upside down for 2 minutes, then invert and let cool. Label and date. Store in a cool, dark place for 6–12 months. Refrigerate after opening for up to 6 weeks.

preparation 30 minutes + overnight soaking ∗ cooking 1 hour 30 minutes

SWEET JAMS AND PRESERVES

Quince conserve

INGREDIENTS

about 5 (4 pounds) medium quinces
¾ cup lemon juice
4⅓ cups sugar, warmed

Put two small plates in the freezer for testing purposes (you may not need the second plate). Cut each quince into quarters then peel, core, and cut into small cubes. Place fruit in a large pan with 8 cups water and the lemon juice. Bring slowly to a boil, then reduce the heat and simmer, covered, for 1 hour, or until the fruit is soft.

Add the sugar and stir over low heat, without boiling, for 5 minutes, or until all the sugar has dissolved.

Return to a boil and boil, stirring often, for 25 minutes. Remove any scum during cooking with a skimmer or slotted spoon. When the conserve falls from a tilted wooden spoon in thick sheets without dripping, start testing for setting point.

Remove from heat, place a little conserve on one of the cold plates, then place in the freezer for 30 seconds. A skin will form on the surface and the conserve will wrinkle when pushed with your finger when setting point is reached. Remove any scum from the surface with a skimmer or slotted spoon.

Spoon immediately into clean, warm jars and seal. Turn the jars upside down for 2 minutes, then invert and let cool. Label and date. Store in a cool, dark place for 6–12 months. Refrigerate after opening for up to 6 weeks.

note QUINCES WILL TURN FROM THEIR NATURAL YELLOW TO A BEAUTIFUL, RICH RED DURING COOKING.

preparation 20 minutes ✦ cooking 1 hour 30 minutes

SWEET JAMS AND PRESERVES

Dried apricot jam

INGREDIENTS
3¼ cups dried apricots
6½ cups sugar, warmed
½ cup slivered almonds

Place the dried apricots in a large nonmetallic bowl. Add 8 cups water and let soak overnight.

Put two small plates in the freezer for testing purposes (you may not need the second plate). Pour the apricots and the water into a large pan. Bring to a boil, then reduce heat and simmer, covered, for 45 minutes, or until the fruit is soft.

Add the sugar and stir over low heat, without boiling, for 5 minutes, or until all the sugar has dissolved. Return to a boil and boil, stirring often, for 20–25 minutes. Remove any scum during cooking with a skimmer or slotted spoon. Stir frequently across the base of the pan to prevent the jam from sticking. When the jam falls from a tilted wooden spoon in thick sheets without dripping, start testing for setting point.

Remove from the heat, place a little jam on one of the cold plates, then place in the freezer for 30 seconds. A skin will form on the surface and the jam will wrinkle when pushed with your finger when setting point is reached. Remove any scum. Add the almonds.

Spoon immediately into clean, warm jars and seal. Turn upside down for 2 minutes, then invert and let cool. Label and date. Store in a cool, dark place for 6–12 months. Refrigerate after opening for up to 6 weeks.

preparation 10 minutes + overnight soaking + cooking 1 hour 10 minutes

GRIDDLE CAKES WITH JAM

1 cup self-rising flour
1 tablespoon superfine sugar
¾ cup milk
1 egg
jam, to serve

Sift the flour, sugar, and a pinch of salt into a large bowl and make a well in the center. Whisk the milk and egg in a pitcher and slowly pour into the well, whisking to form a smooth batter.

Heat a nonstick frying pan over medium heat and brush lightly with melted butter or oil.

Drop level tablespoons of batter into the frying pan, allowing room for spreading (you will probably fit about four griddle cakes in the pan at a time). Cook the griddle cakes for about 30 seconds, or until small bubbles begin to appear on the surface and the underneath has turned golden brown. Turn over and cook the other side.

Transfer to a plate or wire rack to cool, and repeat with the remaining batter. Serve topped with jam, and with whipped cream if desired.

PREPARATION 10 MINUTES
COOKING 15 MINUTES
MAKES ABOUT 25

Tomato and passion fruit jam

INGREDIENTS
16 (4½ pounds) medium tomatoes
1 cup passion fruit pulp (about 10 medium passion fruit)
¼ cup lemon juice
10¾ cups sugar, warmed

Put two small plates in the freezer for testing purposes (you may not need the second plate). Cut a cross at the base of each tomato, place tomatoes in a large bowl, cover with boiling water, then leave for about 30 seconds, or until the skins start to peel away. Transfer to a bowl of icy cold water, remove the skins, then roughly chop the flesh.

Put the passion fruit pulp, lemon juice, tomato, and any juices in a large pan. Bring to a boil, then reduce the heat and simmer for 15 minutes, or until thick and pulpy.

Add the sugar and stir over low heat, without boiling, until all the sugar has dissolved. Return to a boil and boil for 30–40 minutes, stirring often. Remove any scum during cooking with a skimmer or slotted spoon. When the jam falls from a tilted wooden spoon in thick sheets without dripping, start testing for setting point.

Remove from the heat, place a little jam onto one of the cold plates, then place in the freezer for 30 seconds. A skin will form on the surface and the jam will wrinkle when pushed with your finger when setting point is reached. Remove any scum from the surface.

Pour immediately into clean, warm jars, and seal. Turn the jars upside down for 2 minutes, then invert and let cool. Label and date. Store in a cool, dark place for 6–12 months. Refrigerate after opening for up to 6 weeks.

preparation 25 minutes ✳ cooking 1 hour

SWEET JAMS AND PRESERVES

Fig and orange jam

INGREDIENTS

25 (3 pounds) medium fresh figs, chopped

¾ cup orange juice

¼ cup lemon juice

2 tablespoons sweet sherry

4⅓ cups sugar, warmed

Put two small plates in the freezer for testing purposes (you may not need the second plate). Place the figs in a large pan with the orange juice, lemon juice, and the sherry. Bring to a boil, then reduce the heat and simmer for 20 minutes, or until the figs are soft.

Add the sugar and stir over low heat, without boiling, until all the sugar has dissolved. Return to a boil and boil for 20–25 minutes, stirring often. Remove any scum during cooking with a skimmer or slotted spoon. When the jam falls from a tilted wooden spoon in thick sheets without dripping, start testing for setting point.

Remove from the heat, place a little jam on one of the cold plates, then place in the freezer for 30 seconds. A skin will form on the surface and the jam will wrinkle when pushed with your finger when setting point is reached. Remove any scum from the surface with a skimmer or slotted spoon.

Pour immediately into clean, warm jars and seal. Turn the jars upside down for 2 minutes, then invert and let cool. Label and date. Store in a cool, dark place for 6–12 months. Refrigerate after opening for up to 6 weeks.

note EITHER DARK- OR GREEN-SKINNED FIGS CAN BE USED IN THIS RECIPE.

preparation 20 minutes ✦ cooking 50 minutes

MARMALADES AND JELLIES

Red currant jelly

INGREDIENTS
about 5 cups (1¼ pounds) red currants
2¾ cups superfine sugar, warmed

Put two small plates in the freezer for testing purposes (you may not need the second plate). Place the red currants, including stems, and sugar in a pan. Crush the red currants to release the juices. Cook, stirring, over low heat, until all the sugar has dissolved.

Increase the heat and boil rapidly for 5 minutes, stirring often. Remove from the heat, place a little jelly on one of the cold plates, then place in the freezer for 30 seconds. When setting point is reached, a skin will form on the surface and the jelly will wrinkle when pushed with your finger. Skim off any scum with a skimmer or slotted spoon and push the mixture through a fine strainer into a heatproof jug.

Pour immediately into clean, warm jars and seal. Turn the jars upside down for 2 minutes, then invert and let cool. Label and date. Store in a cool, dark place for 6–12 months. Refrigerate jars after opening for up to 6 weeks.

note FOR A SHINY GLAZE AND BEAUTIFUL FINISH ON SWEET FRUIT FLANS, MELT A LITTLE JELLY WITH WATER AND BRUSH OVER THE TOP OF THE FRUIT. OR MELT A SPOONFUL IN SAVORY SAUCES AND GRAVIES.

preparation 20 minutes ✳ cooking 20 minutes

MARMALADES AND JELLIES

Roast turkey *with red currant jelly*

For celebratory occasions, a roast turkey with all the trimmings is the perfect meal and the effort and time that goes into its preparation will be well rewarded with praise.

INGREDIENTS
6¾-pound turkey
1¼ cups butter, softened
1 onion, roughly chopped
4 sage leaves
1 rosemary sprig
½ celery rib, cut into 2–3 pieces
1 medium carrot, cut into 3–4 pieces
1 cup dry white wine
½ cup dry marsala
1 cup chicken broth

red currant jelly (recipe on previous page)

STUFFING
3½ ounces prosciutto, finely chopped
8 ounces ground pork
8 ounces ground chicken
1 egg
⅓ cup heavy cream
⅓ cup chestnut purée
½ teaspoon finely chopped fresh sage
a pinch of cayenne pepper

Preheat the oven to 325°F. Combine all the stuffing ingredients in a bowl, season well with sea salt and freshly ground black pepper, then mix thoroughly.

Fill the turkey with the stuffing and sew up the opening with kitchen string. Cross the legs and tie them together, then tuck the wings behind the body. Rub the skin with ⅓ cup of the butter. Put the onion in the center of a large roasting pan and place the turkey on top, breast side up. Add another 3½ ounces of butter to the pan with the sage, rosemary, celery, and carrot, then pour the wine and marsala over.

Roast for 2½–3 hours, basting several times with the pan juices and covering the turkey breast with buttered parchment paper when the skin becomes golden brown. Transfer the turkey to a large warmed plate, cover loosely with aluminum foil and let rest in a warm place for 30 minutes before carving.

Transfer the vegetables to a food processor and blend until smooth. Add the pan juices and any scrapings from the base of the pan and process until well blended. Transfer to a saucepan, add the remaining butter and broth, then bring to a boil. Season and cook until thickened, then transfer to a serving pitcher.

Serve the turkey with the stuffing, gravy, and red currant jelly.

preparation approximately 40 minutes ✴ cooking 2½-3 hours + 30 minutes resting time before serving ✴ serves 8

Quince jelly

INGREDIENTS
about 10 (4½ pounds) small ripe yellow quinces
¼ cup lemon juice
3 cups superfine sugar, warmed

Wipe the quinces clean, then cut into 2-inch pieces, including the skin and cores. Place the quince pieces in a large pan with 8 cups water. Bring slowly to a boil, then reduce the heat and simmer, covered, for 1 hour, or until tender. Mash any firmer pieces with a masher.

Place a jelly strainer bag in a bowl, cover with boiling water, then drain and suspend the bag over a large heatproof bowl.

Ladle the fruit and liquid into the bag. Do not push the fruit through the bag or the jelly will become cloudy. Cover the top of the bag loosely with a clean dish towel, without touching the fruit mixture. Allow the mixture to drip through the bag overnight, or until there is no liquid dripping through the cloth.

Put two small plates in the freezer for testing purposes (you may not need the second plate). Discard the pulp and measure the liquid. Pour the liquid into a large pan and stir in the lemon juice. Add 1 cup of the warmed sugar for each 1 cup of liquid. Stir over low heat for 5 minutes, or until all the sugar has dissolved. Bring to a boil and boil rapidly for 20–25 minutes, stirring often. Skim any scum during cooking with a skimmer or slotted spoon. Start testing for setting point.

Remove from the heat, place a little jelly on one of the cold plates, the place in the freezer for 30 seconds. When setting point is reached, a skin will form on the surface and the jelly will wrinkle when pushed with your finger. Remove any scum.

Pour immediately into clean, warm jars; seal. Turn upside down for 2 minutes, then invert and let cool. Label and date. Store in a cool, dark place for 6–12 months. Refrigerate after opening for up to 6 weeks.

preparation 20 minutes + overnight draining + cooking 1 hour 30 minutes

Three-fruit marmalade

INGREDIENTS
1 medium grapefruit
2 medium oranges
2 medium lemons
13 cups sugar, warmed

Scrub the fruit under warm, running water with a soft bristle brush to remove the wax coating. Quarter the grapefruit and halve the oranges and lemons, slice them thinly, then place in a nonmetallic bowl. Retain the seeds and place them on a square of cheesecloth and tie securely with string. Add the cheesecloth bag to the bowl with 10 cups water, then cover and leave overnight.

Put two small plates in the freezer for testing purposes (you may not need the second plate). Put the fruit and water in a large pan. Bring to a boil, then reduce the heat and simmer, covered, for 1 hour, or until the fruit is tender.

Add the sugar and stir over low heat, without boiling, for 5 minutes, or until all the sugar has dissolved. Return to a boil and boil rapidly for 50–60 minutes, stirring often. Remove any scum during cooking with a skimmer or slotted spoon. When the marmalade falls from a tilted wooden spoon in thick sheets without dripping, start testing for setting point.

Remove from the heat, place a little marmalade on one of the cold plates, then place in the freezer for 30 seconds. When setting point is reached, a skin will form on the surface and the marmalade will wrinkle when it is pushed with your finger. Discard the bag. Remove any scum from the surface.

Spoon immediately into clean, warm jars, and seal. Turn the jars upside down for 2 minutes, then invert and let cool. Label and date. Store in a cool, dark place for 6–12 months. Refrigerate after opening for up to 6 weeks.

preparation 30 minutes + overnight soaking + cooking 2 hours 5 minutes

MARMALADES AND JELLIES

Seville orange marmalade

INGREDIENTS
4 (about 2½ pounds) medium Seville oranges
4–4½ pounds sugar, warmed

Scrub the oranges under warm, running water with a soft bristle brush to remove any wax coating. Cut the oranges in half, and then in half again. Slice the oranges thinly, removing and retaining the seeds. Place the seeds on a square of cheesecloth and tie securely with a piece of string. Place the oranges and the cheesecloth bag in a large nonmetallic bowl. Cover with 8 cups water and leave overnight.

Put two small plates in the freezer for testing purposes (you may not need the second plate). Place the fruit and cheesecloth bag in a large pan. Bring slowly to a boil, reduce heat and simmer, covered, for 45 minutes, or until the fruit is tender.

Measure fruit and for every 1 cup of the fruit mixture add 1 cup of warmed sugar. Stir over low heat, without boiling, for 5 minutes, or until all the sugar has dissolved. Return to a boil and boil rapidly for 30–40 minutes, stirring often. Remove scum during cooking with a skimmer or slotted spoon. When marmalade falls from a tilted wooden spoon in thick sheets without dripping, start testing for setting point. Remove from the heat, place a little marmalade on one of the cold plates, then place in the freezer for 30 seconds. When setting point is reached, a skin will form on the surface and marmalade will wrinkle when pushed with your finger. Discard the cheesecloth bag. Remove any scum from the surface. Spoon immediately into clean, warm jars and seal. Turn upside down for 2 minutes, then invert and cool. Label and date. Store in a cool, dark place for 6–12 months. Refrigerate after opening for up to 6 weeks.

note SEVILLE ORANGES ARE TROPICAL OR SEMI-TROPICAL FRUITS THAT MAKE GREAT MARMALADE DUE TO THEIR THICK, ROUGH SKIN, AND TART FLESH. THEY ARE GENERALLY ONLY USED IN COOKING.

preparation 30 minutes + overnight soaking ✦ cooking 1 hour 30 minutes

Grape jelly

INGREDIENTS
about 10 cups (4½ pounds) black seedless grapes
⅓ cup lemon juice, reserving any seeds
2¼ cups sugar, warmed

Remove the stems from the grapes. Place the grapes in a large pan and add 1 cup water. Place the lemon seeds on a square of cheesecloth and tie securely with string. Add to the pan. Slowly bring to a boil, then reduce the heat and simmer for 30–35 minutes, or until grapes are soft and pulpy. Remove and discard the cheesecloth bag.

Place a jelly strainer bag in a bowl, cover with boiling water, then drain and suspend the bag over a large heatproof bowl.

Ladle the grape mixture into the jelly strainer bag. Do not push the fruit through the bag or the jelly will turn cloudy. Cover the top of the bag loosely with a clean dish towel, without touching the fruit mixture. Allow the mixture to drip through the bag overnight, or until no liquid drips through the cloth.

Discard the pulp and measure the liquid. Pour the liquid into a stainless steel or enamel pan and stir in the lemon juice. Add ¾ cup sugar for each 1 cup liquid. Stir over a low heat until all the sugar has dissolved, then bring to a boil and boil rapidly, stirring often, for 20–25 minutes, skimming any scum during cooking with a skimmer or slotted spoon.

Transfer to a heatproof pitcher and immediately pour the jelly down the insides of clean, warm jars and seal. Turn the jars upside down for 2 minutes, then invert and let cool. Label and date. Store in a cool, dark place for 6–12 months. Refrigerate after opening for up to 6 weeks.

preparation 15 minutes overnight draining ✳ cooking 1 hour 5 minutes

MARMALADES AND JELLIES

Kumquat marmalade

INGREDIENTS
80 (2¼ pounds) medium kumquats
¼ cup lemon juice
5⅔ cups sugar, warmed

Scrub the kumquats under warm, running water with a soft bristle brush to remove the wax coating. Discard the stems. Halve each lengthways, removing and retaining the seeds, and slice finely. Place the seeds on a square of cheesecloth and tie securely with string. Put the fruit and seeds in a large nonmetallic bowl. Add 5 cups water, cover with plastic wrap and leave overnight.

Put two small plates in the freezer for testing purposes (you may not need the second plate). Place the kumquats and cheesecloth bag in a large pan with the lemon juice. Bring slowly to a boil, then reduce the heat and simmer, covered, for 30 minutes, or until the fruit is tender.

Add the warmed sugar. Stir over low heat, without boiling, for 5 minutes, or until all the sugar has dissolved. Return the mixture to a boil and boil rapidly, stirring frequently, for 20 minutes. Skim any scum from the surface during cooking with a skimmer or slotted spoon. When the marmalade falls from a tilted wooden spoon in thick sheets without dripping, start testing for setting point.

Remove the pan from the heat, place a little marmalade on one of the cold plates, then place in the freezer for 30 seconds. A skin will form on the surface and the marmalade will wrinkle when pushed with your finger when setting point is reached. Discard the cheesecloth bag. Remove any scum from the surface.

Spoon immediately into clean, warm jars. Turn upside down for 2 minutes, then invert and let cool. Label and date. Store in a cool, dark place for 6–12 months. Refrigerate after opening for up to 6 weeks.

preparation 20 minutes + overnight soaking + cooking 1 hour

Pomegranate jelly

INGREDIENTS
about 8 (4–5 pounds) medium pomegranates
3 medium green apples
about 2 cups superfine sugar, warmed
¼ cup lemon juice

Cut the pomegranates in half; use a juicer to squeeze out the juice. At least 2 cups of juice will be needed. (The amount of juice in the fruit varies and, hence, the amount of sugar needed will vary.) Chop the apples; include skin and cores. Place in large pan with pomegranate juice and 1 cup water. Bring slowly to a boil, reduce the heat, then simmer, covered, for 20 minutes, or until the apple is mushy.

Place a jelly strainer bag in a large bowl, cover with boiling water, drain and suspend the bag over a large heatproof bowl. Place a large heatproof bowl under the cloth. Ladle the fruit and liquid into the bag. Do not push the fruit through the bag or the jelly will become cloudy. Cover the top of the bag loosely with a clean dish towel, without touching the fruit mixture. Allow the mixture to drip through the bag overnight, or until there is no liquid dripping through the cloth. Put two small plates in the freezer for testing purposes (you may not need the second plate). Discard the pulp and measure the liquid. Pour the liquid into a large pan. Add 1 cup of sugar for every 1 cup of the liquid and stir over medium heat until all the sugar has dissolved. Stir in the lemon juice. Bring to a boil and boil rapidly for 15–20 minutes, stirring often. Skim the scum off the surface with a skimmer or slotted spoon during cooking. Start testing for setting point.

Remove from the heat, place a little jelly on one of the cold plates, then place in the freezer for 30 seconds. A skin will form on the surface and the jelly will wrinkle when pushed with your finger when setting point is reached. Remove any scum from the surface. Stand the clean, warm jars on a wooden board or a cloth-covered surface. Carefully transfer the jelly to a heatproof pitcher. Wrap the jars in a cloth to protect your hands. Tilt the jar and pour the jelly down the sides of the jars to stop bubbles forming. Seal the jars while hot and gently turn upside down for 2 minutes, then invert and let cool. Label and date. Store in a cool, dark place for 6–12 months. Refrigerate after opening for up to 6 weeks.

preparation 15 minutes + overnight draining＊ cooking 50 minutes

Cointreau orange marmalade

INGREDIENTS
5½ (2¼ pounds) medium oranges
8¼ cups sugar, warmed
⅓ cup Cointreau or other orange-flavored liqueur

Scrub the oranges with a soft bristle brush under warm, running water to remove the wax coating. Cut them in half, then into thin slices, reserving the seeds. Place the seeds on a square of cheesecloth and tie securely with string. Place the orange slices and cheesecloth bag in a large nonmetallic bowl with 8 cups water, then cover and leave overnight.

Put two small plates in the freezer for testing purposes (you may not need the second plate). Transfer the fruit, water, and cheesecloth bag to a large pan. Bring slowly to a boil, then reduce the heat and simmer, covered, for 1 hour, or until the fruit is tender and the mixture has reduced by a third.

Measure the fruit and for every 1 cup of the fruit mixture add 1 cup of warmed sugar. Stir over low heat, without boiling, for 5 minutes, or until all the sugar has dissolved. Bring to a boil and boil rapidly for 40–50 minutes, stirring often. Remove any scum during cooking with a skimmer or slotted spoon. When the marmalade falls from a tilted wooden spoon in thick sheets without dripping, start testing for setting point.

Remove from heat, place a little marmalade on one of the cold plates, then place in freezer for 30 seconds. A skin will form on the surface and marmalade will wrinkle when pushed with your finger when setting point is reached. Discard the cheesecloth bag. Remove scum from the surface. Stir in the Cointreau.

Spoon immediately into clean, warm jars. Turn upside down for 2 minutes, then invert and let cool. Label and date. Store in a cool, dark place for 6–12 months. Refrigerate after opening for up to 6 weeks.

preparation 25 minutes +overnight soaking✻ cooking 2 hours

REFRESHING LIMES

There could be nothing more refreshing
than the smell of a just-cut lime. Use their piquant
juice to flavor drinks such as margaritas and
in dishes such as quacamole and salsa.
Squeeze fresh juice over papaya chunks
and mango to add a bit of zing.

Lime marmalade

INGREDIENTS
17 (2¼ pounds) medium limes
9¾ cups sugar, warmed

Scrub the limes under warm, running water with a soft bristle brush to remove the wax coating. Cut in half lengthways, reserving the seeds, then slice thinly and place in a large nonmetallic bowl with 8 cups water. Tie the lime seeds securely in a square of cheesecloth and add to the bowl. Cover and leave overnight.

Put two small plates in the freezer for testing purposes (you may not need the second plate). Place the fruit and water in a large pan. Bring slowly to a boil, then reduce the heat and simmer, covered, for 45 minutes, or until the fruit is tender. Add the sugar and stir over low heat, without boiling, for 5 minutes, or until all the sugar has dissolved. Return to a boil and boil rapidly, stirring often, for 20 minutes. Remove any scum during cooking with a skimmer or slotted spoon. When the marmalade falls from a tilted wooden spoon in thick sheets without dripping, start testing for setting point.

Remove from heat, place a little marmalade on one of the cold plates, then place in the freezer for 30 seconds. A skin will form on the surface and the marmalade will wrinkle when pushed with your finger when setting point is reached. Discard the cheesecloth bag. Remove any scum from the surface.

Spoon immediately into clean, warm jars. Turn upside down for 2 minutes, then invert and let cool. Label and date. Store in a cool, dark place for 6–12 months. Refrigerate after opening for up to 6 weeks.

note LOOK FOR BRIGHTLY COLORED LIMES THAT FEEL HEAVY FOR THEIR SIZE.

preparation 20 minutes + overnight soaking ∗ cooking 1 hour 10 minutes

Chicken *in tangy lime marmalade sauce*

Stir-frying is the perfect technique for the busy cook. The addition of lime marmalade in this recipe adds an intense depth of flavor to the mild-tasting chicken.

INGREDIENTS

1 pound boneless, skinless chicken thighs, cut into strips

2-inch piece ginger, cut into paper-thin slices

4 scallions, thinly sliced

oil, for cooking

1 red bell pepper, thinly sliced

1 tablespoon mirin (Japanese cooking wine)

1 tablespoon lime marmalade (recipe on previous page)

2 teaspoons shredded lime peel

2 tablespoons lime juice

Put the chicken, ginger, scallions, and some ground black pepper in a dish. Toss well to combine.

Heat a wok until very hot, then add 1 tablespoon of the oil and swirl it around to coat the side. Stir-fry the chicken mixture in three batches over high heat for about 3 minutes, or until golden brown and cooked through. Reheat the wok in between each batch, adding more oil when necessary. Remove all the chicken from the wok and set aside.

Reheat the wok, then add the red pepper and stir-fry for 30 seconds. Add the mirin, marmalade, lime peel, and lime juice, then season with salt and freshly ground black pepper. Cover and steam for 1 minute. Add the chicken and cook, uncovered, for 2 minutes, or until heated through.

Hint CHOOSE YOUNG GINGER WITH THIN SKIN AS IT WILL BE TENDER AND EASY TO SLICE.

preparation 25 minutes ✳ cooking 20 minutes ✳ serves 4

Grapefruit marmalade

INGREDIENTS
3 (2¾ pounds) large grapefruit
2 medium lemons
11 cups sugar, warmed

Scrub the fruit under warm, running water with a soft bristle brush to remove the wax coating. Remove the peel from the fruit in long strips, avoiding the bitter white pith. Cut the strips into 2-inch lengths, then slice thinly. Remove the white pith from the fruit, then chop the flesh, discarding the seeds. Place all the fruit and peel in a large nonmetallic bowl with 10 cups water; cover and leave overnight.

Put two small plates in the freezer for testing purposes (you may not need the second plate). Place the fruit and water in a large pan, bring to a boil, then reduce heat and simmer, covered, for 45 minutes, or until the fruit is tender.

Add the sugar and stir over low heat, without boiling, for 5 minutes, or until all the sugar has dissolved. Return to a boil and boil, stirring often, for 40–50 minutes, checking frequently in the last 20 minutes. Remove any scum during cooking with a skimmer or slotted spoon. When the marmalade falls from a tilted wooden spoon in thick sheets without dripping, start testing for setting point.

Remove from the heat, place a little marmalade on one of the cold plates, then place in the freezer for 30 seconds. A skin will form on the surface and the marmalade will wrinkle when pushed with your finger when setting point is reached. Remove any scum from the surface with a skimmer or slotted spoon.

Spoon immediately into clean, warm jars and seal. Turn the jars upside down for 2 minutes, then invert and let cool. Label and date. Store in a cool, dark place for 6–12 months. Refrigerate after opening for up to 6 weeks.

preparation 30 minutes + overnight soaking + cooking 1 hour 40 minutes

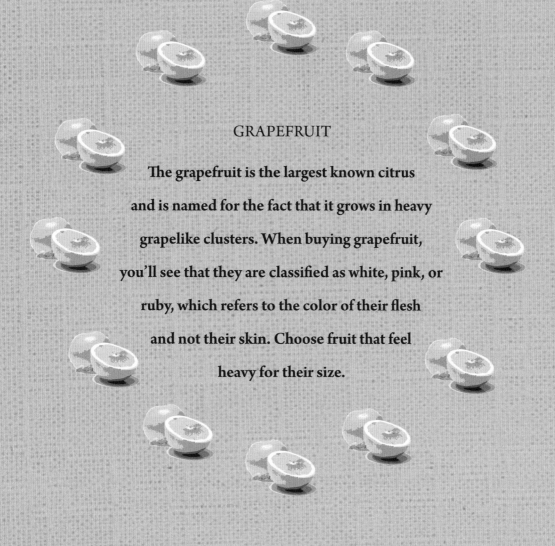

GRAPEFRUIT

The grapefruit is the largest known citrus
and is named for the fact that it grows in heavy
grapelike clusters. When buying grapefruit,
you'll see that they are classified as white, pink, or
ruby, which refers to the color of their flesh
and not their skin. Choose fruit that feel
heavy for their size.

Apple and rose jelly

INGREDIENTS
about 8 (3 pounds 5 ounces) medium apples
2 unsprayed roses
about 1⅓ cups superfine sugar, warmed
2 teaspoons rose water

Chop the apples and put them in a pan with 4 cups water. Cook over a low heat for 45 minutes, or until the apples have broken down into a purée. Place a jelly strainer bag in a bowl, cover with boiling water, then drain and suspend the bag over a large heatproof bowl.

Ladle the purée into the bag. Do not push the fruit through the bag or the jelly will become cloudy. Cover the top of the bag loosely with a clean dish towel, without touching the fruit mixture. Allow the mixture to drip through the bag overnight, or until there is no liquid dripping through the cloth.

Put two small plates in the freezer for testing purposes (you may not need the second plate). Pull the petals off the roses and wash them gently in cold water. Discard the pulp and measure the liquid. Pour the liquid into a large pan and add 1⅓ cups warmed sugar for every 2½ cups liquid. Stir over a low heat until all the sugar has dissolved. Bring to a boil and boil, stirring mixture frequently, for 5–10 minutes. Skim off any scum during cooking with a slotted spoon. Start testing for setting point.

Remove from the heat, place a little jelly on one of the cold plates, then place in the freezer for 30 seconds. A skin will form on the surface and the jelly will wrinkle when pushed with your finger when setting point is reached. Remove any scum from the surface. Stir in rose petals and rose water, then let cool slightly until the jelly is beginning to set (this will ensure that the rose petals are suspended in the jelly).

Pour the jelly down the sides of clean, warm jars and seal. Turn the jars upside down for 10 minutes, then slowly invert them to disperse the petals evenly. Label and date. Store in a cool, dark place for 6–12 months. Refrigerate after opening for up to 6 weeks.

preparation 20 minutes + overnight draining ✦ cooking 1 hour

MARMALADES AND JELLIES

SAVORY JAMS AND PICKLES

Onion and thyme marmalade

INGREDIENTS
about 16 (4½ pounds) medium onions, cut into rings
3 cups malt vinegar
6 black peppercorns
2 bay leaves
3½ cups firmly packed light brown sugar
2 tablespoons fresh thyme leaves
10 x 1¼-inch sprigs fresh thyme

Place the onion in a large pan with the vinegar. Put the peppercorns and bay leaves on a square of cheesecloth and tie securely with string. Add to the pan. Bring to a boil, then reduce the heat and simmer for 40–45 minutes, or until the onion is very soft.

Add the sugar, thyme leaves, and 1 teaspoon salt. Stir until all the sugar has dissolved. Bring to a boil, then reduce the heat and simmer for 20–30 minutes, or until thick and syrupy. Skim any scum off the surface during cooking with a skimmer or slotted spoon. Discard the cheesecloth bag and stir in the thyme sprigs.

Spoon the onion pulp immediately into clean, warm jars, then pour in the syrup and seal the jars. Turn the jars upside down for 2 minutes, then invert and let cool. Label and date. Leave for 1 month before opening to allow the flavors to develop. Store in a cool, dark place for up to 12 months. Refrigerate after opening for up to 6 weeks.

preparation 20 minutes ∗ cooking 1 hour 20 minutes

SAVORY JAMS AND PICKLES

Roast lamb *with onion and thyme marmalade*

Rosemary and lamb are one of the great flavor combinations. Thyme, another resinous herb, makes a great addition to the roast when included in an onion marmalade.

INGREDIENTS

2 rosemary sprigs

3 garlic cloves, chopped

2½ ounces pancetta, chopped

4½-pound leg of lamb, shank bone cut off
 just above joint, trimmed of excess fat, and tied

1 large onion

½ cup olive oil

1½ cups dry white wine

onion and thyme marmalade (see previous page)

Preheat the oven to 450°F. Pull the leaves off the rosemary sprigs. Using a large, sharp knife, chop the rosemary, garlic, and pancetta until a coarse paste forms, then season with sea salt and freshly ground black pepper. Using a small, sharp knife, make incisions ½-inch deep all over the lamb. Then rub the rosemary mixture over the lamb, pushing it into the incisions.

Peel the onion, then cut it widthways into four thick slices and place in the center of a roasting pan. Sit the lamb leg on top, pour the olive oil over, then roast for 15 minutes.

Reduce the oven temperature to 350°F and pour in 1 cup of the wine. Roast for 1¼ hours for medium–rare, or until cooked to your liking, basting from time to time and adding a little water if the juices start to burn. Transfer the lamb to a warm platter, then cover loosely with foil and let rest in a warm place for 10 minutes.

Remove the onion from the roasting pan and spoon off the excess fat. Place the pan over high heat on the stovetop, then pour in the remaining wine and cook for 3–4 minutes, or until the sauce reduces and thickens. Season to taste. Carve the lamb. Arrange on warmed plates and serve with the spooned sauce over the top and with onion and thyme marmalade on the side.

preparation 20 minutes ✳ cooking 1 hour 45 minutes ✳ serves 6

Tomato sauce

INGREDIENTS

20 (5½ pounds) medium, firm, ripe tomatoes

1 large onion

2 teaspoons black peppercorns

2 teaspoons whole cloves

2 teaspoons whole allspice

1½ tablespoons tomato paste

4 garlic cloves, crushed

2 teaspoons ground ginger

¼ teaspoon cayenne pepper

2½ cups white wine or cider vinegar

1 cup sugar

Roughly chop the tomatoes and onion. Place the peppercorns, whole cloves, and allspice on a square of cheesecloth and tie securely with string.

Place the tomato and onion in a large pan with the cheesecloth bag, tomato paste, garlic, ginger, cayenne pepper, vinegar, and 1 teaspoon salt. Bring slowly to a boil, reduce the heat and simmer for 45 minutes. Add the sugar and stir over low heat for 5 minutes, or until all the sugar has dissolved. Bring to a boil, then reduce the heat and simmer for 1 hour, or until the sauce is thick and pulpy. Stir frequently during cooking and watch that the mixture does not burn. Discard the cheesecloth bag.

Place the mixture in a coarse strainer set over a large bowl, in batches if necessary. Use a metal spoon to press all the juices firmly from the pulp. Discard the pulp and return the juice to the clean pan. Gently reheat the mixture for 10 minutes, then pour immediately into clean, warm jars or bottles and seal. Turn the jars upside down for 2 minutes, then invert them and let cool. Label and date. Leave for 1 month before opening to allow the flavors to develop. Store in a cool, dark place for up to 12 months. Refrigerate after opening for up to 6 weeks.

preparation 25 minutes ✦ cooking 2 hours

Sausage rolls *with tomato sauce*

A firm favorite in lunch boxes, as party fare or as a meal with a salad, every good sausage roll deserves a dollop of top-quality tomato sauce.

INGREDIENTS
3 sheets frozen puff pastry, thawed
2 eggs, lightly beaten
1 pound 10 ounces ground sausage meat
1 onion, finely chopped
1 garlic clove, crushed
1 cup fresh bread crumbs
3 tablespoons chopped Italian parsley
3 tablespoons chopped thyme

½ teaspoon ground sage
½ teaspoon freshly shredded nutmeg
½ teaspoon ground cloves
tomato sauce (recipe on previous page)

Preheat the oven to 400°F. Lightly grease two cookie sheets.

Cut the pastry sheets in half and lightly brush the edges with some of the beaten egg.

Mix half the remaining egg with the remaining ingredients and ½ teaspoon black pepper in a large bowl, then divide into six even portions. Pipe or spoon the filling down the center of each piece of pastry, then brush the edges with some of the egg. Fold the pastry over the filling, overlapping the edges and placing the join underneath. Brush the rolls with more egg, then cut each into six short pieces.

Cut two small slashes on top of each roll, then place on the cookie sheets and bake for 15 minutes. Reduce the heat to 350°F and bake for another 15 minutes, or until puffed and golden. Place the tomato sauce in a pitcher and serve alongside.

preparation 30 minutes ✦ cooking 30 minutes ✦ makes 36

Preserved lemons

INGREDIENTS
8–12 small thin-skinned lemons
1 cup rock salt
2 cups lemon juice (8–10 lemons)
½ teaspoon black peppercorns
1 bay leaf
1 tablespoon olive oil

Scrub the lemons under warm running water with a soft bristle brush to remove the wax coating. Cut into quarters, leaving the base attached at the stem end. Gently open each lemon, remove any visible seeds and pack 1 tablespoon of the salt against the cut edges of each lemon. Push the lemons back into shape and pack tightly into a 8-cup jar with a clip or tight-fitting lid. (Depending on the size of the lemons, you may not need all 12. They should be firmly packed and fill the jar.)

Add 1 cup of the lemon juice, the remaining rock salt, the peppercorns, and bay leaf to the jar. Fill the jar to the top with the remaining lemon juice. Seal and shake to combine all the ingredients. Leave in a cool, dark place for 6 weeks, inverting each week. (In warm weather, store in the refrigerator.) The liquid will be cloudy initially, but will clear by the fourth week.

To test if the lemons are preserved, cut through the center of one of the lemon quarters. If the pith is still white, the lemons are not ready. Re-seal and leave for another week before testing again.

Once the lemons are preserved, cover the brine with a layer of olive oil. Replace the oil each time you remove some of the lemon.

note SERVE THE LEMONS WITH BROILED MEATS OR USE TO FLAVOR COUSCOUS, STUFFINGS, TAGINES, AND CASSEROLES. ONLY THE PEEL IS USED IN COOKING. DISCARD THE FLESH, RINSE, THEN FINELY SLICE OR CHOP THE PEEL BEFORE ADDING TO THE DISH.

preparation 1 hour + 6 weeks standing ✳ no cooking required

SAVORY JAMS AND PICKLES

Chicken with olives *and preserved lemons*

This is one of the classic dishes of Morocco, where preserved lemons are frequently used. Use unpitted olives; if bitter, blanch in boiling water for 5 minutes before use.

INGREDIENTS

¼ cup olive oil

3½-pound chicken

1 onion, chopped

2 garlic cloves, chopped

2½ cups chicken broth

½ teaspoon ground ginger

1½ teaspoons ground cinnamon

pinch saffron threads

heaping ½ cup green olives

¼ preserved lemon, pulp removed, zest washed and cut into slivers (recipe on previous page)

2 bay leaves

2 chicken livers

3 tablespoons chopped cilantro leaves

Preheat the oven to 350°F. Heat 2 tablespoons of the oil in a large frying pan, then add the chicken and brown on all sides. Place in a deep flameproof casserole dish. Heat the remaining oil in the pan, then add the onion and garlic and cook over medium heat for 3–4 minutes, or until softened. Add the broth, ginger, cinnamon, saffron, olives, lemon, and bay leaves and pour around the chicken. Bake for 45 minutes, or until the juices run clear when the thigh is pierced with a skewer, adding a little more water or broth if the sauce gets too dry.

Remove the chicken from the casserole dish, then cover with foil and let rest. Put the dish on the stove over medium heat, add the chicken livers and mash into the sauce as they cook. Cook for 5–6 minutes, or until the sauce has reduced and thickened. Add the chopped cilantro. Cut the chicken into four pieces and serve with the sauce.

preparation 10 minutes ✳ cooking 1 hour ✳ serves 4

SAVORY JAMS AND PICKLES

Indian lime pickle

INGREDIENTS
10 firm yellow/pale green limes
¾ cup oil
1 teaspoon fenugreek seeds
¾ teaspoon ground turmeric
3 teaspoons chili powder
1 teaspoon asafoetida powder

Wash the limes and dry thoroughly. Heat ¼ cup oil in a pan. Add 2 limes and cook over low heat, turning often, for 2 minutes. Remove and repeat until all the limes are done. Do not allow the skin to turn brown. Cool, then cut each lime into eight wedges and cut each wedge into three. Discard the seeds and reserve any juice.

In a dry pan, heat the fenugreek seeds for 1 minute, or until the color lightens. Take care not to burn the seeds as this will make the pickle bitter. Grind to a fine powder in a mortar and pestle or spice mill.

Heat the remaining oil in a heavy-bottomed pan. Add the turmeric, chili powder, asafoetida, and 1 tablespoon salt. Stir quickly then add the limes and reserved juice. Turn off the heat, add the ground fenugreek and stir well.

Spoon immediately into clean, warm jars. Pour a thin layer of warmed oil into each bottle. Seal, label, and date. Leave for 1 month before opening to allow the flavors to develop. Store in a cool, dark place for up to 12 months. Refrigerate after opening for up to 6 weeks.

note DARK GREEN LIMES ARE TOO ACIDIC SO USE PALE GREEN/YELLOW ONES. THE PEEL SOFTENS WITH TIME. ASAFOETIDA POWDER IS A DRIED PLANT RESIN WITH A VERY PUNGENT GARLICKY SMELL. IT IS AVAILABLE FROM INDIAN SPICE STORES.

preparation 20 minutes + cooling + cooking 15 minutes

Fried beef kerala *with Indian lime pickle*

Pickles are very much a part of an Indian meal and, generally, two or three types will be served along with a dish of chilled yogurt to cool the spiciness of the meal.

INGREDIENTS

oil, for deep-frying, plus 2 tablespoons oil

1 medium potato, cut into small cubes

1 pound 2 ounces sirloin steak, thinly sliced

3 garlic cloves, crushed

1 teaspoon ground black pepper

2-inch piece of ginger, shredded with a fine grater into a bowl, placed in a piece of cheesecloth and squeezed to produce 1 tablespoon juice

2 medium onions, sliced in rings

¼ cup beef broth

2 tablespoons tomato paste

2 teaspoons soy sauce

1 teaspoon chili powder

¼ cup lemon juice

3 medium tomatoes, chopped

½ cup fresh or frozen peas

Indian lime pickle (recipe on previous page)

Fill a deep, heavy-bottomed saucepan one-third full with oil and heat it to 350°F, or until a cube of bread browns in 15 seconds. Deep-fry the potato until golden brown. Drain on kitchen paper.

Put the steak in a bowl and toss with the garlic, pepper, and ginger juice. Heat the extra oil and fry the beef quickly in batches over high heat. Keep each batch warm as you remove it. Reduce the heat and fry the onion until golden, then remove.

Cook the beef broth, tomato paste, soy sauce, chili, and lemon juice in the pan over medium heat until reduced. Add the onion, cook for 3 minutes, stir in the tomato and peas, then cook for 1 minute. Add the beef and potato and toss until heated through. Serve with Indian lime pickle.

preparation 15 minutes * cooking 30 minutes * serves 4

SAVORY JAMS AND PICKLES

Thai sweet chili sauce

INGREDIENTS

13 (5 ounces) medium–large fresh red chilies

1⅔ cups golden raisins

3 garlic cloves, chopped

1½-inch piece fresh ginger, finely shredded

1 cup white vinegar

1⅔ cups sugar

⅔ cup firmly packed light brown sugar

1 tablespoon fish sauce

Wearing latex or rubber gloves to protect your hands, cut the chilies in half and remove the seeds.

Combine the chili, golden raisins, garlic, ginger, and ¼ cup of the vinegar in a food processor or blender and process until smooth.

Place the chili mixture in a large pan, stir in the remaining vinegar, white and brown sugar, fish sauce, ¼ teaspoon salt, and 5 tablespoons water. Bring the mixture to a boil, stirring until all the sugar has dissolved, then reduce the heat and simmer, stirring often, for 15 minutes, or until the mixture is a slightly thick, syrupy consistency.

Pour immediately into clean, warm jars or bottles and seal. Turn the jars upside down for 2 minutes, then invert and cool. Label and date. Leave for 1 month before opening to allow the flavors to develop. Store in a cool, dark place for up to 12 months. Refrigerate after opening for up to 6 weeks.

note THIS SAUCE IS QUITE SWEET, YET HAS A GOOD BITE. IF YOU PREFER A MILDER SAUCE, YOU CAN ADJUST THE AMOUNT OF CHILI TO YOUR TASTE. THE SEEDS CONTAIN THE MOST HEAT, SO REMEMBER TO REMOVE THESE. WEARING GLOVES HELPS PREVENT ANY IRRITATION TO SENSITIVE SKIN, WHICH CAN SOMETIMES OCCUR WHEN HANDLING CHILIES.

preparation 30 minutes ✻ cooking 20 minutes

SAVORY JAMS AND PICKLES

Shrimp omelets *with Thai sweet chili sauce*

Creamy little omelets filled with sweet shrimp meat and flavored with cilantro and chili make a simple but special dish. The sauce adds an extra hit of chili.

INGREDIENTS

1 pound 2 ounces raw shrimps

1½ tablespoons oil

4 eggs, lightly beaten

2 tablespoons fish sauce

8 scallions, chopped

6 cilantro roots, chopped

2 garlic cloves, chopped

1 small red chili, seeded and
    chopped

2 teaspoons lime juice

2 teaspoons shredded jaggery
    or light brown sugar

3 tablespoons chopped cilantro leaves

1 small red chili, extra, chopped,
    to garnish

cilantro sprigs, to garnish

Thai sweet chili sauce (recipe on previous page)

Peel the shrimps, gently pull out the dark vein from each shrimp back, starting from the head end, then chop the shrimp meat.

Heat a wok over high heat, add 2 teaspoons of the oil and swirl to coat. Combine the egg with half of the fish sauce. Add 2 tablespoons of the mixture to the wok and swirl to a 6-inch round. Cook for 1 minute, then gently lift out. Repeat with the remaining egg mixture to make eight omelets.

Heat the remaining oil in the wok. Add the shrimps, scallion, cilantro root, garlic, and chili. Stir-fry for 3–4 minutes, or until the shrimps are cooked. Stir in the lime juice, jaggery, cilantro leaves, and the remaining fish sauce.

Divide the shrimp mixture among the omelets and fold each into a small firm parcel. Cut a slit in the top and garnish with the chili and cilantro sprigs. Serve with Thai sweet chili sauce.

preparation 25 minutes ✦ cooking 15 minutes ✦ makes 8

Green tomato pickles

INGREDIENTS

10 (2¾ pounds) medium green tomatoes

2 onions

½ cup cooking salt

1 cup sugar

2 cups cider vinegar

½ cup golden raisins

½ teaspoon pumpkin pie spice

½ teaspoon ground cinnamon

2 teaspoons curry powder

pinch cayenne pepper

2 teaspoons cornstarch

Slice the tomatoes and onions into thin rounds. Combine them with salt in a large nonmetallic bowl, then add enough water to cover. Place a small plate on top of the vegetables to keep them submerged. Leave overnight.

Drain the tomato and onion and rinse well. Place in a large pan and add the sugar, vinegar, golden raisins, and spices. Stir over low heat for 5 minutes, or until all the sugar has dissolved. Bring to a boil, then reduce the heat and simmer for 30 minutes, stirring often, or until the vegetables are soft.

Add 2 teaspoons water to the cornstarch, then mix well and stir into the mixture. Stir over medium heat until it boils and thickens.

Spoon immediately into clean, warm jars and seal. Turn the jars upside down for 2 minutes, then invert and let cool. Label and date. Leave for 1 month before opening to allow the flavors to develop. Store in a cool, dark place for up to 12 months. Refrigerate after opening for up to 6 weeks.

preparation 25 minutes + overnight soaking ✳ cooking 40 minutes

RED OR GREEN?

Green tomatoes are those at the end of the
season, which will fail to fully ripen in the
cooling weather. Firm, not as juicy as their
ripe counterparts, and piquant-tasting, green
tomatoes make excellent relishes and chutneys.
Their suitability for frying is legendary.

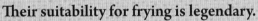

Okra pickles

INGREDIENTS

1⅔ cups cider vinegar

1 teaspoon coriander seeds

1 teaspoon mustard seeds

1 cinnamon stick

4–6 dried small red chilies

2 tablespoons light brown sugar

1 onion, chopped

about 75 (1 pound) small okra, chopped into
½-inch pieces

Place the vinegar, spices, chilies, sugar, and 1½ tablespoons water in a large pan and bring to a boil. Reduce the heat and simmer for 5 minutes, then remove from the heat, cover, and infuse for 25 minutes.

Strain the vinegar mixture, reserving the chilies, then return to the pan. You will need about 1½ cups of liquid. Add the onion, okra, and 2 tablespoons salt and bring to a boil. Reduce the heat and simmer over a low heat for 5 minutes, or until the okra is half cooked and there is no more of the sliminess that the okra releases. Skim off any scum during cooking with a skimmer or slotted spoon.

Strain the okra and onion mixture, reserving the liquid, and pack immediately into clean, warm jars, adding two of the reserved chilies to each jar. Fill the jars with the reserved pickling liquid and seal. Turn upside down for 2 minutes, then invert and let cool. Label and date. Leave for 1 month before opening to allow the flavors to develop. Store in a cool, dark place for up to 12 months. Refrigerate after opening for up to 6 weeks.

note USE SMALL OKRA AS THE LARGER, OLDER ONES TEND TO BE MORE FIBROUS. THE OKRA WILL START TO ABSORB THE LIQUID AFTER 1–2 WEEKS.

preparation 20 minutes + 25 minutes standing ✳ cooking 10 minutes

SAVORY JAMS AND PICKLES

Plum sauce

INGREDIENTS

1 large green apple

2 red chilies

16 (2½ pounds) medium blood plums, halved

2 cups firmly packed light brown sugar

1½ cups white wine vinegar

1 onion, shredded

¼ cup soy sauce

2 tablespoons fresh ginger, finely chopped

2 garlic cloves, crushed

Peel, then core and chop the apple and place in a large pan with ½ cup water. Cover and simmer for 10 minutes, or until the apple is soft. Cut the chilies in half lengthways. Remove the seeds and chop finely. Add the plums, sugar, vinegar, onion, soy sauce, ginger, garlic, and the chili.

Bring the mixture to a boil and cook, uncovered, over low–medium heat for 45 minutes. Stir the mixture often throughout the cooking process. Remove the sauce from the pan and press it through a coarse strainer set over a large bowl using a wooden spoon. Discard the plum seeds. Rinse the pan. Put the sauce back in the clean pan and return to the heat.

Cook the sauce rapidly while stirring until it has thickened slightly—it will thicken even more on cooling.

Pour immediately into clean, warm jars and seal. Turn the jars upside down for 2 minutes, then invert and let cool. Label and date. Leave for 1 month before opening to allow the flavors to develop. Store in a cool, dark place for up to 12 months. Refrigerate after opening for up to 6 weeks.

preparation 20 minutes + cooking 1 hour

Spring rolls *with plum sauce*

It is worth making the effort to cook spring rolls from scratch. The wrappers can be purchased from Asian supermarkets. A good plum sauce is an essential accompaniment.

INGREDIENTS

2 dried shiitake mushrooms

9 ounces ground pork

1½ tablespoons dark soy sauce

2 teaspoons dry sherry

½ teaspoon Chinese five-spice

2 tablespoons cornstarch, plus
    1½ teaspoons, extra

⅓ cup peanut oil

½ celery rib, finely chopped

2 scallions, thinly sliced

1 ounce canned bamboo shoots, finely sliced

¾ cup shredded Chinese cabbage

2 garlic cloves, crushed

2 teaspoons finely chopped fresh ginger

¼ teaspoon sugar

¼ teaspoon sesame oil

9-ounce packet 4½-inch square spring roll
    wrappers

oil, for deep-frying

plum sauce (recipe on previous page)

Put the shiitake mushrooms in a heatproof bowl, cover with boiling water, and soak for 20 minutes. Squeeze the mushrooms dry, then discard the stems and thinly slice the caps. Mix the pork, soy sauce, sherry, five-spice, and 1 tablespoon of the cornstarch in a nonmetallic bowl and leave for 15 minutes.

Heat 2 tablespoons of the peanut oil in a wok over high heat until nearly smoking, then add the celery, scallion, bamboo shoots, and Chinese cabbage and stir-fry for 3–4 minutes, or until just soft. Season with salt, then transfer to a bowl and set aside. Heat the remaining peanut oil in the wok and cook the garlic and ginger for 30 seconds. Add the pork mixture and stir-fry for 2–3 minutes, or until nearly cooked. Combine 1½ teaspoons of the cornstarch with ¼ cup water. Return the cooked vegetables to the wok, then stir in mushrooms. Add the sugar, sesame oil, and cornstarch mixture and stir for 2 minutes. Remove from the heat and cool.

Make a paste with the remaining cornstarch and 2–3 teaspoons cold water. Place a spring roll wrapper on a work surface, with one corner pointing toward you. Put 2 teaspoons of the filling in the center of the wrapper, then brush the edges with a little cornstarch paste. Roll up, tucking in the sides as you do so. Repeat with the remaining filling and wrappers. Fill a wok or deep heavy-bottomed saucepan one-third full of oil and heat to 350°F, or until a cube of bread dropped into the oil browns in 15 seconds. Deep-fry the spring rolls in batches until golden, then drain on crumpled kitchen paper. Serve hot with the plum sauce.

preparation 45 minutes ✴ cooking 20 minutes ✴ makes 30

Chili and garlic sauce

INGREDIENTS
8 large dried chilies
4 medium fresh red chilies
4 garlic cloves
½ cup white vinegar
¾ cup sugar
1 tablespoon fish sauce

Remove the stem and seeds from the dried chilies, and break into large pieces. Place in a bowl, then cover with boiling water, and soak for 15 minutes.

Meanwhile, cut the fresh chilies in half and remove the seeds. Wear gloves to protect your hands. Finely chop the garlic. Drain the dried chili and place in a food processor or blender with the fresh chili and vinegar and process until smooth.

Pour into a pan and bring to a boil, then reduce the heat, stir in the sugar and garlic, and simmer for 10 minutes, stirring often, until slightly thickened. Add the fish sauce.

Transfer to a heatproof pitcher and pour immediately into clean, warm jars and seal. Turn the jars upside down for 2 minutes, then invert and cool. Label and date. Leave for 1 month before opening to allow the flavors to develop. Store in a cool, dark place for up to 12 months. Refrigerate after opening.

note THE HEAT IN THE CHILI DEPENDS ON THE CHILIES USED AND THEIR SIZE. USUALLY, THE SMALLER THE CHILI, THE HOTTER IT IS.

preparation 20 minutes + 15 minutes soaking + cooking 15 minutes

SAVORY JAMS AND PICKLES

Zucchini patties *with chili and garlic sauce*

Zucchini is an under-valued vegetable that is more versatile than many cooks realize. These delicious patties go well with a pungent chili and garlic sauce.

INGREDIENTS

2¼ cups shredded zucchini (about 4 zucchini)

1 small onion, finely chopped

¼ cup self-rising flour

⅓ cup freshly shredded kefalotyri
   or Parmesan cheese

1 tablespoon chopped mint

2 teaspoons chopped Italian parsley

pinch freshly ground nutmeg

¼ cup dry bread crumbs

1 egg, lightly beaten

olive oil, for pan-frying

lemon wedges, to serve

chili and garlic sauce (recipe on previous page)

Put the zucchini and onion in the center of a clean dish towel, then gather the corners together and twist as tightly as possible to remove all the juices. Combine the zucchini, onion, flour, cheese, mint, parsley, nutmeg, bread crumbs, and egg in a large bowl. Season well, then mix with your hands to form a stiff mixture that clumps together.

Heat the oil in a large frying pan over medium heat. When hot, drop level tablespoons of mixture into the pan and pan-fry for 2–3 minutes, or until well browned all over. Drain well on crumpled kitchen paper and serve hot, with lemon wedges and the chili and garlic sauce.

preparation 20 minutes ✦ cooking 15 minutes ✦ makes 16

SAVORY JAMS AND PICKLES

Red pepper sauce

INGREDIENTS

3 (4½ pounds) medium red bell peppers

2 medium tomatoes

1 large onion, chopped

1 small green apple, peeled, cored and chopped

¾ cup firmly packed light brown sugar

2 cups cider vinegar

2 teaspoons black peppercorns

2 tablespoons roughly chopped fresh basil leaves

1 teaspoon cloves

1 bay leaf

3 garlic cloves

Preheat the oven to 400°F. Roast the bell peppers for 35 minutes, or until the skin blisters and blackens. Cut into quarters, then remove the skins, seeds, and membrane, and chop the flesh.

Score a cross in the base of each tomato. Place in a heatproof bowl and cover with boiling water. Leave for 30 seconds, then transfer to cold water and peel the skin away from the cross. Roughly chop the flesh.

Put the bell pepper, tomato, onion, and apple in a food processor or blender and process until finely chopped. Place in a large pan with the sugar, vinegar, and 1 teaspoon salt. Put the peppercorns, basil, cloves, bay leaf, and garlic on a square piece of cheesecloth, tie with string and add to the pan.

Stir over low heat until all the sugar has dissolved. Bring to a boil, then reduce heat and simmer, stirring often, over low–medium heat, for 1 hour 15 minutes, or until the sauce is thick and pulpy. Process in a food processor or blender until smooth.

Pour immediately into clean, warm bottles or jars and seal. Turn upside down for 2 minutes, then invert and let cool. Label and date. Leave for 1 month before opening to allow the flavors to develop. Store in a cool, dark place for up to 12 months. Refrigerate after opening.

preparation 30 minutes ✳ cooking 2 hours

Eggplant pickle

INGREDIENTS

2 eggplants, cut into ½-inch cubes

4 garlic cloves, chopped

¼ cup chopped fresh ginger

2 red chilies, chopped

½ cup oil

1 medium onion, chopped

1 tablespoon ground cumin

1 teaspoon fennel seeds

1 tablespoon ground coriander

½ teaspoon ground turmeric

1 cup white wine vinegar

⅔ cup sugar

Put the eggplant in a colander set over a bowl and sprinkle with 1 tablespoon salt. Leave for 20 minutes, then rinse well in cold water and pat dry with kitchen paper. Chop the garlic, ginger, and chili in a food processor, adding a teaspoon of water if necessary, to make a paste.

Heat the oil in a large pan, add the onion, and cook for 2 minutes, or until soft. Add the garlic paste and the ground cumin, fennel seeds, ground coriander, and turmeric, then cook, stirring, for 1 minute. Add the eggplant and cook for 5–10 minutes, or until the eggplant has softened.

Add the white wine vinegar, sugar, and 1 teaspoon salt, if necessary, and stir to combine. Cover and simmer gently for 15 minutes, or until soft.

Spoon the pickle immediately into clean, warm jars. Use a skewer to remove any air bubbles, then seal. Turn the jars upside down for 2 minutes, then invert them and let cool. Label and date. Leave for 1 month to allow the flavors to develop. Store the jars in a cool, dark place for up to 12 months. Refrigerate after opening for up to 6 weeks.

preparation 20 minutes + 20 minutes standing time + cooking 30 minutes

CHUTNEYS AND RELISHES

Spicy dried fruit chutney

INGREDIENTS

2½ cups dried apricots

1⅓ cups dried peaches

1 cup dried pears

1½ cups raisins

1¼ cups pitted dates

2 medium onions

2 small or 1 large green apple(s), peeled and cored

4 garlic cloves, finely chopped

1 teaspoon ground cumin

1 teaspoon ground coriander

1 teaspoon ground cloves

1 teaspoon ground cayenne pepper

2¾ cups lightly packed light brown sugar

2½ cups malt vinegar

Finely chop the apricots, peaches, pears, raisins, dates, onions, and apples. Place in a large pan. Add the garlic, cumin, coriander, cloves, cayenne pepper, sugar, vinegar, 2 teaspoons salt, and 3 cups water.

Stir over low heat until all the sugar has dissolved. Increase the heat and bring to a boil, then reduce the heat and simmer, stirring often, over medium heat for 1½ hours, or until the mixture has thickened and the fruit is soft and pulpy. Do not cook over high heat because the liquid will evaporate too quickly and the flavors will not have time to fully develop.

Spoon immediately into clean, warm jars, then seal. Turn upside down for 2 minutes, then invert and let cool. Label and date. Leave for 1 month before opening to allow the flavors to develop. Store in a cool, dark place for up to 12 months. Refrigerate after opening.

preparation 20 minutes ✳ cooking 1 hour 35 minutes

THE KING OF FRUITS

There are about 350 varieties of mangoes.
Hayden has particularly juicy flesh, its orange
skin blushing to red when ripe. Green-skinned
mangoes are hard and are a popular ingredient in
Southeast Asian salads, pickles, and chutneys.
Their flesh can be coarsely shredded or cut
off the stone in thick slices.

Green mango chutney

INGREDIENTS

6 (5¾ pounds) medium firm green
   mangoes

1 large onion, finely chopped

⅔ cup white vinegar

½ cup firmly packed light brown sugar

¾ cup sugar

2 teaspoons ground ginger

2 teaspoons garam marsala

Remove the peel from the mangoes. Cut the cheeks from the rounded side of each mango and the small amount of flesh around the sides of the seed. Chop flesh into ½-inch pieces and place in a large pan.

Add the remaining ingredients and 1 teaspoon salt to the pan. Stir over medium heat, without boiling, for 5 minutes, or until all the sugar has dissolved.

Bring to a boil, then reduce the heat and simmer for about 45 minutes, or until the mixture is very thick and pulpy. Stir often during cooking to prevent the chutney from sticking and burning on the bottom, especially toward the end of the cooking time.

Spoon immediately into clean, warm jars and seal. Turn the jars upside down for 2 minutes, then invert and let cool. Label and date. Leave for 1 month before opening to allow the flavors to develop. Store in a cool, dark place for up to 12 months. Refrigerate after opening for up to 6 weeks.

note THIS CHUTNEY IS A TRADITIONAL ACCOMPANIMENT TO INDIAN-STYLE DISHES. CHOOSE FIRM, GREEN MANGOES WITHOUT BRUISES OR BLEMISHES.

preparation 20 minutes ✳ cooking 50 minutes

CHUTNEYS AND RELISHES

Pork vindaloo *with green mango chutney*

Vindaloo is notorious for being hot and spicy. It was invented by the Portuguese in Goa. The tart, fruity chutney is a suitably lively accompaniment.

INGREDIENTS

2¼-pound leg of pork on the bone

6 cardamom pods

1 teaspoon black peppercorns

4 dried chilies

1 teaspoon cloves

4-inch cinnamon stick, roughly broken

1 teaspoon cumin seeds

½ teaspoon ground turmeric

½ teaspoon coriander seeds

¼ teaspoon fenugreek seeds

4 tablespoons clear vinegar

1 tablespoon dark vinegar

4 tablespoons oil

2 medium onions, finely sliced

10 garlic cloves, finely sliced

2-inch piece of ginger, cut into matchsticks

3 medium ripe tomatoes, roughly chopped

4 green chilies, chopped

1 teaspoon jaggery or light brown sugar

green mango chutney (recipe on previous page)

Trim away any excess fat from the pork, then remove the bone and cut the pork flesh into 1-inch cubes. Reserve the bone.

Split open the cardamom pods and remove the seeds. Finely grind the cardamom seeds, peppercorns, dried chilies, cloves, cinnamon stick, cumin seeds, turmeric, coriander seeds, and fenugreek seeds in a spice grinder or mortar and pestle.

In a large bowl, mix the ground spices with the vinegars. Add the pork and mix thoroughly to coat well. Cover and marinate in the fridge for 3 hours.

Heat the oil in a casserole over low heat and fry the onion until lightly browned. Add the garlic, ginger, tomato, and chili, and stir well. Add the pork, increase the heat to high, and fry for 3–5 minutes, or until browned. Add 1 cup water and any of the marinade liquid left in the bowl, then reduce the heat and bring slowly back to a boil. Add the jaggery and the pork bone. Cover tightly and simmer for about 1½ hours, stirring occasionally until the meat is very tender. Discard the bone. Season with salt, to taste. Serve with pickle on the side.

preparation 20 minutes + 3 hours marinating * cooking 1 hour 50 minutes * serves 4

Chow chow

INGREDIENTS

1½-pound cauliflower, cut into small florets

1 small cucumber, peeled, seeded and cut into
    ¾-inch cubes

3 cups sliced green beans

1 medium red and 1 medium green bell pepper, cut into cubes

4 cups cider vinegar

1 cup firmly packed light brown sugar

2 tablespoons mustard powder

2 tablespoons yellow mustard seeds

2 teaspoons ground turmeric

pinch cayenne pepper

½ cup all-purpose flour

14-oz can red kidney beans, rinsed and drained

1½ cups canned corn kernels, drained

Blanch the cauliflower florets, cucumber, beans, and peppers separately in boiling water. Drain and cool quickly under cold running water. Set aside.

Reserve 1 cup of the vinegar. Combine the remaining vinegar with the sugar, mustard powder, mustard seeds, turmeric, and cayenne pepper in a large pan. Stir over low heat to dissolve the sugar.

Whisk the reserved vinegar and the flour together in a bowl. Add to the pan and whisk over medium heat for 5 minutes, or until the mixture boils and thickens. Add the blanched vegetables, kidney beans, and corn kernels. Mix thoroughly, bring to a boil, and cook, stirring often, for another 5 minutes.

Spoon immediately into clean, warm jars and seal. Turn upside down for 2 minutes, then invert and let cool. Label and date. Leave for 1 month before opening to allow the flavors to develop. Store in a cool, dark place for up to 12 months. Refrigerate after opening for up to 6 weeks.

preparation 30 minutes + cooking 20 minutes

Nectarine and lemongrass chutney

INGREDIENTS

3 large green chilies

3 stalks lemongrass, white part only

10 (3¼ pounds) medium nectarines, pits removed, roughly chopped

3 garlic cloves, finely chopped

2 tablespoons shredded fresh ginger

1 large onion, chopped

2 teaspoons ground coriander

2 cups white wine vinegar

1½ cups lightly packed light brown sugar

Cut the chilies in half, then remove the seeds from two and finely slice all the chilies. Bruise the lemongrass with the back of a knife and slice finely.

Place all the ingredients in a large pan and add 1 teaspoon salt. Stir over low heat for 5 minutes, or until all the sugar has dissolved.

Bring to a boil, then reduce the heat and simmer for 45–50 minutes, or until the chutney is thick and pulpy. Stir often to prevent the chutney from sticking or burning on the bottom.

Spoon immediately into clean, warm jars and seal. Turn the jars upside down for 2 minutes, then invert and let cool. Label and date. Leave for 1 month before opening to allow the flavors to develop. Store in a cool, dark place for up to 12 months. Refrigerate after opening for up to 6 weeks.

note IT IS BEST TO WEAR GLOVES WHEN HANDLING CHILIES TO PROTECT YOUR FINGERS FROM THE HEAT OF THE SEEDS AND FLESH.

preparation 25 minutes + cooking 1 hour

CHUTNEYS AND RELISHES

Chili and red pepper relish

INGREDIENTS
4 large red bell peppers
2 large onions, roughly chopped
1 red chili
2 garlic cloves
2 cups white vinegar
about 6½ cups sugar

Quarter the peppers and remove the seeds and white membrane. Roughly chop the flesh and place in a food processor or blender with the onion, chili, garlic, and some salt. You may need to do this in batches. Process until smooth and place in a large pan.

Add the vinegar, bring to a boil and boil for 10–15 minutes, or until tender. Measure the pepper mixture and measure an equal amount of sugar. Add the sugar, stirring until all the sugar has dissolved, and then slowly bring to a boil. Brush down the sides of the pan with a wet brush to remove any undissolved sugar crystals. Remove any scum during cooking with a skimmer or slotted spoon.

Boil for 15 minutes, stirring often, then reduce the heat and simmer for 30 minutes, or until the relish is thick and pulpy.

Spoon immediately into clean, warm jars and seal. Turn the jars upside down for 2 minutes, then invert and cool. Label and date. Leave for 1 month before opening to allow the flavors to develop. Store in a cool, dark place for up to 12 months. Refrigerate after opening for up to 6 weeks.

note BRUSHING THE SIDES OF THE PAN DISSOLVES ANY SUGAR CRYSTALS, WHICH, IF LEFT, COULD CAUSE THE RELISH TO CRYSTALLIZE WHEN CHILLED.

preparation 15 minutes * cooking 1 hour

Banana, tamarind, and date chutney

INGREDIENTS

heaping ¾ cup tamarind pulp

¼ cup superfine sugar

1 teaspoon ground cumin

½ teaspoon cayenne pepper

2 tablespoons shredded fresh ginger

1½ cups pitted dates, chopped

½ cup slivered almonds

8 firm ripe bananas, chopped

Put the tamarind pulp in a bowl with 3 cups boiling water. Cool, then break up with a fork. Pour into a strainer placed over a bowl and press out the liquid. Discard the seeds.

Put the liquid in a large pan with the sugar, cumin, cayenne pepper, and 1 teaspoon salt. Stir over low heat until all the sugar has dissolved.

Add the ginger, dates, and almonds. Bring to a boil, then reduce the heat and simmer for 10 minutes. Add the banana and cook, stirring often, for 30 minutes, or until soft and pulpy.

Spoon the chutney immediately into clean, warm jars. Use a metal skewer to remove any air bubbles and seal. Turn upside down for 2 minutes, then invert and let cool. Label and date. Leave for 1 month before opening to allow the flavors to develop. Store in a cool, dark place for up to 12 months. Refrigerate after opening for up to 6 weeks.

note TAMARIND PULP IS AVAILABLE IN MOST ASIAN GROCERY STORES.

preparation 25 minutes ✦ cooking 45 minutes

Banana Tamarind & Date Chutney

Blueberry relish

INGREDIENTS

6½ cups (2¼ pounds) blueberries

2 cups sugar

¾ cup white wine vinegar

1 teaspoon cayenne pepper

½ teaspoon ground allspice (pimento)

¼ teaspoon ground cinnamon

¼ cup lemon juice (reserve any seeds
    and peel)

Place the blueberries in a large pan with the sugar, vinegar, cayenne pepper, allspice, cinnamon, lemon juice, 1 teaspoon salt, and ½ cup water. Roughly chop the peel of half a lemon and, with the seeds, place on a square of cheesecloth and tie securely with string. Add to the pan. Stir over low heat for 5 minutes, or until all the sugar has dissolved.

Bring to a boil, then reduce the heat and simmer, stirring often, for 50–55 minutes, or until the relish is thick and syrupy.

Spoon immediately into clean, warm jars and seal. Turn the jars upside down for 2 minutes, then invert and let cool. Label and date. Leave for 1 month before opening to allow the flavors to develop. Store in a cool, dark place for up to 12 months. Refrigerate after opening for up to 6 weeks.

note BLUEBERRIES ARE VERY DELICATE FRUIT, SO BE CAREFUL NOT TO OVERCOOK THEM OR THEY WILL BREAK UP AND FALL APART.

preparation 15 minutes + cooking 1 hour

Roast peach chutney

INGREDIENTS

13 (4½ pounds) medium slipstone peaches (choose ripe ones)

2 medium onions, thinly sliced

2 garlic cloves, crushed

1½ cups sugar

2½ cups cider vinegar

1 tablespoon yellow mustard seeds

2 cinnamon sticks

1 teaspoon ground ginger

Preheat the oven to 415°F. Score a cross in the base of each peach. Place the peaches in a heatproof bowl and cover with boiling water. Leave for 30 seconds, then cover with cold water and peel the skin away from the cross. Cut the peaches in half and remove the stone.

Line two to three rectangular pans with parchment paper. Place the peaches in a single layer on the paper and roast for 30 minutes, or until they start to brown on the edges. (A lot of juice will come out of the peaches.) Tip the peaches and any juices into a large pan, and add the onion, garlic, sugar, vinegar, mustard seeds, cinnamon sticks, and ginger. Stir over heat until all the sugar has dissolved.

Return to a boil, then reduce the heat and simmer for 1¼–1½ hours, or until chutney is thick and pulpy. Stir occasionally to break up the peaches and prevent the mixture from sticking to the bottom of the pan. Remove the cinnamon sticks.

Spoon immediately into clean, warm jars and seal. Turn upside down for 2 minutes, then invert and let cool. Label and date. Leave for 1 month before opening to allow the flavors to develop. Store in a cool, dark place for up to 12 months. Refrigerate after opening for up to 6 weeks.

preparation 30 minutes * cooking 2 hours

CHUTNEYS AND RELISHES

Red pepper relish

INGREDIENTS

4 (2¼ pounds) medium red bell peppers

1½ cups red wine vinegar

2 teaspoons black mustard seeds

2 medium red onions, thinly sliced

4 garlic cloves, chopped

1 teaspoon shredded fresh ginger

2 medium green apples, peeled, cored, and
   shredded

1 teaspoon black peppercorns

1 cup firmly packed light brown sugar

Remove the seeds and membranes and thinly slice the peppers. Put in a large pan with the vinegar, mustard seeds, onion, garlic, ginger, and apple. Place the peppercorns on a square of cheesecloth, then tie securely with string and add to the pan. Simmer for 30 minutes, or until the pepper is soft.

Add the sugar and stir over low heat, without boiling, until all the sugar has dissolved. Bring to a boil, stirring often, then reduce the heat and simmer for 1¼ hours, or until the relish is thick and pulpy. Discard the cheesecloth bag.

Spoon immediately into clean, warm jars and seal. Turn the jars upside down for 2 minutes, then invert; cool. Label and date. Leave for 1 month before opening to allow the flavors to develop. Store in a cool, dark place for up to 12 months. Refrigerate after opening for up to 6 weeks.

preparation 40 minutes ✦ cooking 1 hour 50 minutes

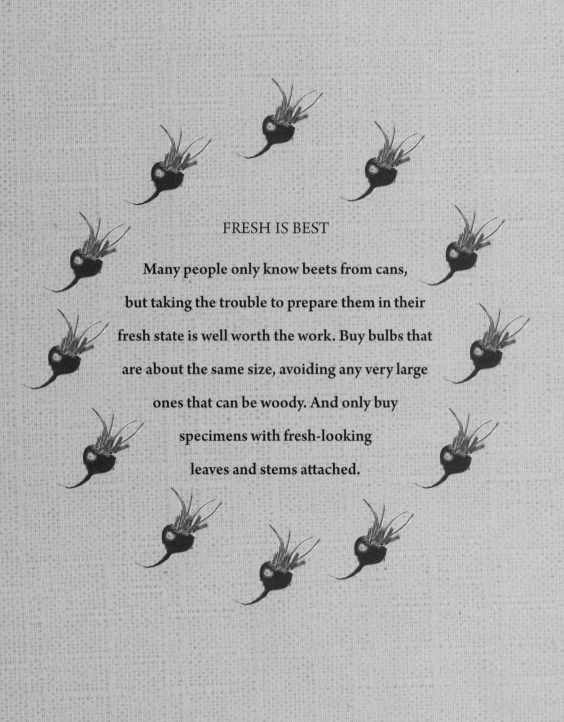

FRESH IS BEST

Many people only know beets from cans, but taking the trouble to prepare them in their fresh state is well worth the work. Buy bulbs that are about the same size, avoiding any very large ones that can be woody. And only buy specimens with fresh-looking leaves and stems attached.

Beet relish

INGREDIENTS

5⅓ cups peeled and coarsely shredded fresh beet (about 1 pound 10 ounces
    beet)

1 medium onion, chopped

2 medium green apples, peeled, cored, and chopped

1⅔ cups white wine vinegar

½ cup lightly packed light brown sugar

½ cup sugar

2 tablespoons lemon juice

Place all the ingredients and 2 teaspoons salt in a large pan and stir over low heat, without boiling, until all the sugar has dissolved. Bring to a boil and boil, stirring often, for 20–30 minutes, or until the beet and onion are tender and the relish is reduced and thickened.

Spoon immediately into clean, warm jars and seal. Turn upside down for 2 minutes, then invert and let cool. Label and date. Leave for 1 month before opening to allow the flavors to develop. Store in a cool, dark place for up to 12 months. Refrigerate after opening for up to 6 weeks.

preparation 25 minutes ✳ cooking 35 minutes

CHUTNEYS AND RELISHES

Spicy squash chutney

INGREDIENTS

6½ cups peeled and chopped squash

2 tablespoons oil

2 teaspoons cumin seeds

½ teaspoon ground cinnamon

½ teaspoon ground coriander

1 onion, chopped

2 garlic cloves, crushed

½ cup golden raisins

⅓ cup firmly packed light brown sugar

½ cup malt vinegar

¾ cup orange juice

1 tablespoon chopped fresh cilantro leaves

Preheat the oven to 400°F. Place the squash in a baking pan and drizzle with the oil. Bake for 40 minutes.

Put the squash and the remaining ingredients, except the cilantro leaves, in a large pan. Add ½ teaspoon salt and bring the mixture to a boil. Reduce the heat and simmer for 10–15 minutes, stirring often, or until the mixture thickens.

Gently stir in the cilantro and remove from the heat. Spoon immediately into clean, warm jars and seal. Turn upside down for 2 minutes, then invert and let cool. Label and date. Leave for 1 month before opening to allow the flavors to develop. Store in a cool, dark place for up to 12 months. Refrigerate after opening for up to 6 weeks.

note TO GET A THICK AND CHUNKY MIXTURE, USE HARDER SQUASH VARIETIES THAT TAKE LONGER TO COOK.

preparation 20 minutes ✳ cooking 55 minutes

Pineapple chutney

INGREDIENTS

1 medium pineapple (choose a ripe one)

2 medium onions, chopped

½ teaspoon ground ginger

½ teaspoon ground cloves

1 teaspoon ground cinnamon

¾ cup firmly packed light brown sugar

½ cup white wine vinegar

½ cup raisins

Peel the pineapple and remove the tough eyes. Cut into quarters, then remove and discard the hard center core and dice the flesh. Combine with the onion, ginger, cloves, cinnamon, sugar, vinegar, and raisins in a large pan and stir over low heat until all the sugar has dissolved.

Bring the mixture to a boil, then reduce the heat and simmer for 1½ hours, stirring often, until the mixture has reduced and thickened and the pineapple is soft.

Spoon immediately into clean, warm jars and seal. Turn the jars upside down for 2 minutes, then invert and let cool. Label and date. Leave for 1 month before opening to allow flavors to develop. Store in a cool, dark place for up to 12 months. Refrigerate after opening for up to 6 weeks.

note THE PINEAPPLE IS RIPE IF IT HAS A FRAGRANT PINEAPPLE AROMA AND THE CENTRAL LEAF PULLS OUT EASILY.

preparation 30 minutes * cooking 1 hour 35 minutes

CHUTNEYS AND RELISHES

Autumn chutney

INGREDIENTS
2 medium pears, peeled, cored, and chopped (choose firm ones)

2½ medium green apples, peeled, cored, and chopped

4 medium tomatoes, peeled and chopped

4 medium onions, chopped

5 celery ribs, sliced

3 garlic cloves, thinly sliced

2 teaspoons shredded fresh ginger

3¾ cups golden raisins

4 cups white vinegar

2 teaspoons ground cinnamon

2 teaspoons ground ginger

2 cups lightly packed light brown sugar

Combine all the ingredients, except the sugar, in a large pan. Bring to a boil, then reduce the heat and simmer for 45 minutes.

Add the sugar and stir until all the sugar has dissolved. Bring to a boil and cook for 30–35 minutes, stirring often, or until the chutney has reduced and thickened.

Spoon the chutney immediately into clean, warm jars and seal. Turn upside down for 2 minutes, then invert and let cool. Label and date. Leave for 1 month before opening to allow the flavors to fully develop. Store in a cool, dark place for up to 12 months. Refrigerate after opening.

preparation 25 minutes ✷ cooking 1 hour 25 minutes

Piccalilli

INGREDIENTS

3¼ cups cauliflower florets

1 small cucumber, chopped

1⅔ cups sliced green beans

1 onion, chopped

2 medium carrots, chopped

2 celery ribs, chopped

⅓ cup salt

1 cup sugar

1 tablespoon mustard powder

2 teaspoons ground turmeric

1 teaspoon ground ginger

1 fresh red chili, seeded and finely chopped

4 cups white vinegar

1⅓ cups frozen fava beans, thawed and peeled

½ cup all-purpose flour

Combine the cauliflower, cucumber, green beans, onion, carrot, celery, and salt in a large bowl. Add enough water to cover the vegetables, and top with a small upturned plate to keep the vegetables submerged. Let soak overnight.

Drain the vegetables well and rinse under cold running water. Drain the vegetables again. Combine the vegetable mixture with the sugar, mustard, turmeric, ginger, chili, and all but ¾ cup of the vinegar in a large pan. Bring to a boil, then reduce the heat and simmer for 3 minutes. Stir in the fava beans. Remove any scum from the surface with a skimmer or slotted spoon.

Blend the flour with the remaining vinegar and stir it into the vegetable mixture. Stir until the mixture boils and thickens. Spoon immediately into clean, warm jars and seal. Turn the jars upside down for 2 minutes, then invert. Label and date. Leave for 1 month before opening to allow the flavors to develop. Store in a cool, dark place for up to 12 months. Refrigerate after opening for up to 6 weeks.

preparation 30 minutes + overnight soaking + cooking 10 minutes

CHUTNEYS AND RELISHES

Roasted tomato relish

INGREDIENTS

16 medium tomatoes, halved

2 medium onions, chopped

2 small red chilies, seeded and chopped

1 teaspoon paprika or Hungarian smoked paprika

1⅓ cups white wine vinegar

1⅓ cups sugar

¼ cup lemon juice

1 teaspoon shredded lemon peel

Preheat the oven to 300°F. Line a cookie sheet with foil and then parchment paper. Place the tomato halves cut-side-up on the cookie sheet and cook for 1 hour. Sprinkle with the onion and cook for another hour.

Cool slightly, then remove the tomato skins and roughly chop the flesh. Place the tomato, onion, chili, paprika, vinegar, sugar, lemon juice, lemon peel, and 2 teaspoons salt into a large pan and stir until all the sugar has dissolved.

Bring to a boil, then reduce the heat and simmer for 45 minutes, or until the relish is thick and pulpy. Stir often to prevent the relish from burning or sticking.

Spoon immediately into clean, warm jars and seal. Turn the jars upside down for 2 minutes, then invert and let cool. Label and date. Leave for 1 month before opening to allow the flavors to develop. Store in a cool, dark place for up to 12 months. Refrigerate after opening for up to 6 weeks.

note IF AVAILABLE, HUNGARIAN SMOKED PAPRIKA GIVES THIS RELISH A LOVELY SMOKY FLAVOR. IT IS AVAILABLE AT SPECIALTY SPICE SHOPS AND DELICATESSENS.

preparation 20 minutes ✳ cooking 2 hours 50 minutes

Cheese-filled crepes *with tomato relish*

The unfilled crepes can be made up to three days in advance but must be refrigerated with parchment paper to separate them.

INGREDIENTS

CREPES

1⅓ cups all-purpose flour

2 cups milk

3 eggs, lightly beaten

1½ tablespoons butter, melted

CHEESE FILLING

1⅔ cups ricotta cheese, crumbled

⅔ cup shredded mozzarella cheese

¼ cup freshly shredded Parmesan cheese

pinch freshly ground nutmeg

3 tablespoons chopped Italian parsley

roasted tomato relish (recipe on previous page)

¼ cup freshly shredded Parmesan cheese

2 tablespoons extra virgin olive oil, to drizzle

To make the crepes, sift the flour and ½ teaspoon salt into a bowl. Make a well in the center and add the milk gradually, stirring constantly until the mixture is smooth. Add the eggs, little by little, beating well until smooth. Cover and set aside for 30 minutes.

Heat a crepe pan or nonstick frying pan and brush lightly with the melted butter. Pour ¼ cup of batter into the pan, swirling quickly to thinly cover the base. Cook for 1 minute, or until the underside is golden. Turn and cook the other side until golden. Transfer to a plate and continue with the remaining batter, stacking the crepes as you go.

Preheat the oven to 400°F and lightly grease a shallow ovenproof dish with butter or oil.

To make the filling, mix all the ingredients together and season well.

To assemble, spread 1 heaping tablespoon of filling over each crepe, leaving a ½-inch border. Fold the crepe in half and then in quarters. Place in the ovenproof dish, so that they overlap but are not crowded. Spoon the tomato sauce over the crepes, then sprinkle with Parmesan and drizzle with the extra virgin olive oil. Bake for 20 minutes, or until heated.

preparation 25 minutes * cooking 1 hour 10 minutes * makes about 12

Traditional chili jam

INGREDIENTS

8 large dried red chilies

2 whole heads of garlic

about 12 (10 ounces) medium red Asian or French shallots

1 cup peanut oil

3½-oz packet small dried shrimps

1 teaspoon shrimp paste

heaping ¾ cup shredded jaggery

3 tablespoons tamarind concentrate

2 teaspoons finely shredded lime peel

Remove the stems and seeds from the chilies and break into large pieces. Place in a bowl, then cover with hot water and soak for 15 minutes. Divide the garlic into cloves. Peel and thinly slice the garlic and shallots. Drain the chili and pat dry.

Heat half the oil in a wok over a medium–low heat and gently fry the garlic, shallots, and chili, stirring often, until golden brown. Remove and drain on kitchen paper.

Place the shrimp in a spice mill, food processor, or mortar and pestle and process or pound until fine. Add the shrimp paste and fried garlic, shallots, and chili, then process to a smooth paste.

Reheat the wok and add the remaining oil and the paste mixture. Cook for 5 minutes, stirring, or until it is very aromatic. Stir in the jaggery, tamarind, lime peel, 1 teaspoon salt, and 5 tablespoons water. Bring to a boil, stirring constantly, for 5–8 minutes, or until the mixture has thickened. Take care not to burn the bottom of the pan. Spoon immediately into clean, warm jars and seal. Store the chili jam in a cool, dark place for 6–12 months. Refrigerate after opening for up to 6 weeks.

note THIS JAM IS THICK AND PASTE-LIKE AND WILL FIRM ON COOLING. INGREDIENTS SUCH AS DRIED SHRIMPS, SHRIMP PASTE, JAGGERY, AND TAMARIND CONCENTRATE ARE AVAILABLE FROM ASIAN FOOD STORES.

preparation 20 minutes + 15 minutes soaking ✦ cooking 20 minutes

CHUTNEYS AND RELISHES

Dried apricot chutney

INGREDIENTS

3¼ cups dried apricots

1 large onion, chopped

3 garlic cloves, finely chopped

2 tablespoons shredded fresh ginger

2 cups cider vinegar

1 cup firmly packed light brown sugar

1 cup golden raisins

2 teaspoons mustard seeds, crushed (see Note)

2 teaspoons coriander seeds, crushed

½ teaspoon ground cumin

⅓ cup orange juice

½ teaspoon shredded orange peel

Put the apricots in a bowl, then cover with 8 cups water and let soak for 2 hours. Drain and put 4 cups of the soaking water into a large pan. Make up the amount with fresh water if there is not enough. Chop the apricots. Put the apricots and all the ingredients, except the orange juice and peel, into the pan. Add 1 teaspoon salt.

Stir the mixture over low heat for 5 minutes, or until all the sugar has dissolved. Bring to a boil, cover and boil for 45 minutes, or until thick and pulpy. Stir often, especially toward the end of the cooking time so the mixture does not stick and burn. Remove any scum during cooking with a skimmer or slotted spoon.

Stir in the orange juice and peel. Spoon immediately into clean, warm jars. Use a skewer to remove any air bubbles, then seal. Turn upside down for 2 minutes, then invert and let cool. Label and date. Leave for 1 month to allow the flavors to develop. Store in a cool, dark place for up to 12 months. Refrigerate after opening for up to 6 weeks.

note CRUSHING THE MUSTARD AND CORIANDER SEEDS HELPS TO RELEASE THEIR AROMA. YOU CAN USE THE BACK OF A LARGE, HEAVY KNIFE TO CRUSH THE SEEDS, OR A MORTAR AND PESTLE, OR PUT THEM IN A THICK PLASTIC BAG AND CRUSH THEM WITH A ROLLING PIN.

preparation 20 minutes + 2 hours soaking ∗ cooking 50 minutes

Sweet corn relish

INGREDIENTS

1 green pepper, seeded and finely
   chopped

1 red pepper, seeded and finely
   chopped

3 x 14-ounce cans whole-kernel corn, drained

1 tablespoon yellow mustard seeds, crushed
   (see Note)

2 teaspoons celery seeds, crushed

1 large onion, finely chopped

2½ cups white wine or cider vinegar

2 tablespoons mustard powder

1 cup firmly packed light brown sugar

1 teaspoon ground turmeric

2 tablespoons cornstarch

Place all the ingredients, except the cornstarch, in a large pan. Add 1 teaspoon salt and stir over low heat for 5 minutes, or until all the sugar has dissolved. Simmer for 50 minutes, stirring frequently.

Combine the cornstarch with 2 tablespoons water. Add to the pan and cook, stirring, for 2–3 minutes, or until the mixture boils and thickens.

Spoon immediately into clean, warm jars. Use a skewer to remove air bubbles and seal. Turn the jars upside down for 2 minutes, then invert and let cool. Label and date. Leave for 1 month before opening to allow the flavors to develop. Store in a cool, dark place for up to 12 months. Refrigerate after opening.

note CRUSH THE MUSTARD AND CELERY SEEDS IN A MORTAR AND PESTLE, OR PLACE IN A PLASTIC BAG AND CRUSH WITH A ROLLING PIN, TO RELEASE THE AROMA.

preparation 15 minutes ✳ cooking 1 hour

CHUTNEYS AND RELISHES

Apple, date, and pecan chutney

INGREDIENTS

2 medium brown onions, chopped

6 (2 pounds 11 ounces) medium green apples, peeled, cored and chopped into small chunks

2½ cups dates, seeded and chopped

1 cup pecans, chopped

2 teaspoons cumin seeds

2 teaspoons finely chopped fresh ginger

1¼ cups white vinegar

½ cup sugar

Put onion and ½ cup water in a large pan. Bring to a boil, then reduce heat and simmer, covered, for 10–15 minutes, or until onion is soft. Add the apple, and simmer, covered, for 15–20 minutes, or until the apple has softened. Stir often.

Add the dates, pecans, cumin seeds, ginger, vinegar, sugar, ½ teaspoon salt, and ¼ cup water. Stir over low heat for 5 minutes, or until all the sugar has dissolved. Simmer for 5 minutes, or until thick.

Spoon immediately into clean, warm jars. Use a skewer to remove any air bubbles, then seal. Turn upside down for 2 minutes, then invert and let cool. Label and date. Leave for 1 month before opening to allow the flavors to develop. Store in a cool, dark place for up to 12 months. Refrigerate after opening for up to 6 weeks. Serve with roast pork, ham, cold meats, and cheese.

preparation 20 minutes ✱ cooking 45 minutes

Sweet tomato and eggplant chutney

INGREDIENTS

16 (4½ pounds) medium ripe tomatoes

4 medium brown onions, chopped

about 8 (1 pound 2 ounces) slender eggplants, finely chopped

4 garlic cloves, finely chopped

2 teaspoons sweet paprika

2 teaspoons brown mustard seeds, crushed

2 cups sugar

2½ cups white vinegar

Score a cross in the base of each tomato, then place four to five at a time in a heatproof bowl and cover with boiling water. Leave for 30 seconds then transfer to cold water and peel the skin away from the cross. Roughly chop the flesh and place in a large pan.

Add the remaining ingredients to the pan. Add 2 teaspoons salt and stir over low heat for 5 minutes, or until all the sugar has dissolved. Bring to a boil, then reduce heat and simmer, for 50–60 minutes, or until the chutney is thick and pulpy. Stir often. Remove any scum during cooking with a skimmer or slotted spoon. Do not cook the mixture over high heat or the liquid will evaporate too quickly and the flavors won't have sufficient time to develop.

Transfer to a heatproof jug and immediately pour into clean, warm jars and seal. Turn the jars upside down for 2 minutes, then invert and let cool. Label and date. Leave for 1 month before opening to allow the flavors to develop. Store in a cool, dark place for up to 12 months. Refrigerate after opening for up to 6 weeks. Serve with cold meats, steak, chicken or fish.

note TO ACHIEVE THE RICHEST FLAVOR, IT IS BEST TO CHOOSE VERY RIPE TOMATOES FOR THIS RECIPE.

preparation 20 minutes ✳ cooking 1 hour 10 minutes

CHUTNEYS AND RELISHES

Mostarda di fruta

INGREDIENTS

heaping ¾ cup candied fruit

1 teaspoon cornstarch

1¼ cups white wine

1 tablespoon honey

3 cloves

1 tablespoon yellow mustard seeds

¼ teaspoon ground nutmeg

½ teaspoon shredded fresh ginger

2 cinnamon sticks, broken into pieces

1 tablespoon lemon juice

Using a pair of scissors, chop the fruit into even-sized pieces. Mix the cornstarch with 1 teaspoon water and blend to a paste.

Place 6½ fluid ounces of water in a pan with the wine, honey, cloves, mustard seeds, nutmeg, ginger, and cinnamon sticks. Bring to a boil, then add the cornstarch mixture. Simmer for 5 minutes, or until the mixture thickens.

Add the candied fruit and lemon juice, and simmer for 10–15 minutes, or until the fruit is soft and the mixture is thick. Spoon immediately into clean, warm jars and seal. Turn upside down for 2 minutes, then invert and let cool. Label and date. Store for a week before eating.

note MOSTARDA DI FRUTA IS POPULAR IN ITALIAN CUISINE. IT IS SERVED WITH COLD MEATS, POULTRY, AND GAME, AND HAS A VERY SWEET FLAVOR.

preparation 10 minutes * cooking 20 minutes

Tomato and chili relish

INGREDIENTS

8 (2 pounds) medium tomatoes

3 medium green apples, peeled, cored, and shredded

2 medium onions, chopped

1 teaspoon shredded fresh ginger

4 garlic cloves, chopped

1–2 long red chilies, sliced

1 cup firmly packed light brown sugar

1 cup cider vinegar

Cut a cross at the base of each tomato, place in a large bowl, then cover with boiling water and leave for 30 seconds, or until the skins start to spilt. Transfer to a bowl of cold water. Peel away the skin, then roughly chop the tomatoes and place in a large pan.

Add the remaining ingredients to the pan and stir over low heat until all the sugar has dissolved. Bring to a boil, then reduce the heat and simmer, stirring often, for 2–2¼ hours, or until the relish has reduced and thickened.

Spoon immediately into clean, warm jars and seal. Turn the jars upside down for 2 minutes, then invert and let cool. Label and date. Leave for 1 month before opening to allow the flavors to develop. Store in a cool, dark place for up to 12 months. Refrigerate after opening for up to 6 weeks.

preparation 20 minutes ✳ cooking 2 hours 20 minutes

CHUTNEYS AND RELISHES

Dried fruits

Dried fruits make a simple, yet delicious, snack to nibble on instead of chips or candy. You can also use crisp dried fruits, lightly dusted with confectioners' sugar, as a garnish on a fruit mousse. Most fruits can be dried, except berries and those with a high water content. It is important to keep dried fruits cool and dry, otherwise they will discolor or go moldy. They can be kept in an airtight container in a cool, dry place for up to 2 weeks.

Before you start the drying process, think about how you are going to slice the fruit to make it look its best. Apples, for example, are best sliced across the middle, while pears are best sliced lengthways. Fruit such as rhubarb can be shaped during the cooling process.

A mandolin is a hand-held slicer with extremely sharp, adjustable blades. Always use the safety shield when slicing. If you have one, a mandolin will make slicing some of the smaller fruit much easier. If you don't have a mandolin, you need a good, sharp knife, so be careful! You can pick the fruit you wish to dry because of its shape, for example, carambola. Adding lemon juice helps the fruit keep its color, as does the sugar, but check your fruit regularly while it is drying to make sure it doesn't burn or get too brown. Cool any fruit thoroughly before storing it in an airtight container—it should keep for a few days before softening but can be quickly refreshed in the oven until it dries out again.

PINEAPPLE
Peel and remove the tough eyes from a medium-sized pineapple, then cut the flesh into ⅛-inch slices. Pat the slices dry with kitchen paper and spread them out on cookie sheets lined with baking parchment. Sprinkle the pineapple slices lightly with sugar and cook in an oven at the lowest possible temperature for 3 hours. Turn the slices over approximately halfway through the cooking process. Check every now and then to make sure the pineapple pieces don't get too dark or burn. Remove the pineapple carefully from the cookie sheets when dry, then cool completely before storing in an airtight container.

APPLES AND PEARS
Slice 2 medium apples and 2 medium pears as thinly as you can, about ⅛-inch thick, if possible, leaving the skin and core intact. Cut the apples through the middle to get a pretty star-shaped pattern from the core. Cut the pears through their length. Put both the apple and pear slices in a bowl, sprinkle them with a little lemon juice and toss to coat thoroughly. Pat the fruit slices dry with kitchen paper and spread out on cookie sheets lined with baking parchment. Sprinkle the apple and pear slices lightly with sugar and cook in an oven at the lowest possible temperature for 2½–3 hours. Turn the slices over approximately halfway through the cooking process. Check now and then to make sure fruit pieces don't get too dark or burn. Remove carefully from the tray when dry. Cool completely before storing in an airtight container.

CARAMBOLA

Cut 2 or 3 carambolas into ⅛-inch slices and sprinkle with the juice of half a lemon. Pat the carambola slices dry with kitchen paper and spread out on cookie sheets lined with baking parchment. Sprinkle lightly with sugar and cook in an oven at the lowest possible temperature for 2–2½ hours. Turn the slices over approximately halfway through the cooking process. Check every now and then to make sure they don't get too dark or burn. Remove the carambola carefully from the tray when dry and cool completely before storing in an airtight container.

RHUBARB

Remove the string and trim the ends from 2 or 3 rhubarb stems and slice into long, thin strips along the length of the fruit. Pat rhubarb slices dry with kitchen paper and spread out on cookie sheets lined with baking parchment. Sprinkle lightly with sugar. Cook in an oven at the lowest possible temperature for 2½ –3 hours. Turn the slices over approximately halfway through the cooking process. Check every now and then to make sure the rhubarb pieces don't get too dark or burn. Remove the rhubarb carefully from the tray when dry and then cool completely before storing in an airtight container. If you want to be creative, you can try wrapping the cooked rhubarb around the handle of a wooden spoon when cooling.

note TO KEEP THE FRUIT AS CRISP AS POSSIBLE, SPREAD A THIN LAYER OF UNCOOKED RICE ON THE BASE OF AN AIRTIGHT CONTAINER, THEN COVER WITH BAKING PARCHMENT AND TOP WITH THE FRUIT. THE RICE WILL ABSORB ANY EXCESS MOISTURE. DRYING TIMES MAY VARY GREATLY, DEPENDING ON THE FRUIT CHOSEN, THE SEASON AND OVEN TEMPERATURES. ONCE OPENED, REFRIGERATE FOR 1–2 WEEKS.

Curds

Fruit curds are delicious spread on toast, biscuits, croissants, or griddle cakes. They can also be used as fillings for sponge cakes, crêpes, flans, or meringues. When placed in decorated jars, they always make popular gifts. Or, pour into small jars, then label, date, and sell at your next school bake sale. The mixture of fruit and butter gives a rich, creamy consistency and taste that is hard to resist. They will keep for up to 2 months in the refrigerator, should they not get eaten well before then.

LEMON CURD

Combine 1½ tablespoons finely shredded lemon peel, ¾ cup soft unsalted butter, ¾ cup lemon juice, and 1 cup superfine sugar in a heatproof bowl. Place the bowl over a pan of gently simmering water, without touching the water, and stir the mixture until the butter has melted and all the sugar has dissolved. Add 12 egg yolks and stir constantly until the mixture thickens and coats the back of a spoon. This will take about 15–20 minutes—the heat must remain low or the mixture will curdle. Strain the mixture, reheat, and then pour into clean, warm jars. Seal while hot, then label and date. Keep in the refrigerator for up to 2 months. Makes about 2½ cups.

MANGO AND LIME CURD

Cut the cheeks from 2 large mangoes, cutting on either side of the stone, then peel and chop the flesh. Blend the flesh in a food processor or blender until smooth. Push through a fine strainer. You will need 1¼ cups of strained mango purée. Combine the purée with ½ teaspoon finely shredded lime peel, ⅓ cup strained lime juice, ⅔ cup soft unsalted butter, 1 cup sugar, and 4 beaten eggs in a heatproof bowl. Place the bowl over a pan of simmering water, without touching the water. Stir constantly until the butter has melted and the sugar has dissolved. Stir for 15–20 minutes, or until the mixture thickens and coats the back of a spoon. Remove from the heat, then pour into clean, warm jars and seal while hot. Keep in refrigerator for up to 2 months. Makes about 3½ cups.

PASSION FRUIT CURD

Beat 4 eggs and strain them into a heatproof bowl. Stir in ¾ cup superfine sugar, ⅓ cup lemon juice, ¾ cup soft butter, ½ cup passion fruit pulp, and 3 teaspoons shredded lemon peel. Place the bowl over a pan of simmering water, without letting it touch the water, and stir until the butter has melted and the sugar has dissolved. Stir constantly for 15–20 minutes, or until the mixture thickly coats the back of a spoon. Spoon into clean, warm jars. Seal while hot. Refrigerate when cool. Keep in the refrigerator for up to 2 months. Makes 2½ cups.

VANILLA BEAN AND LEMON CURD

Place 2 teaspoons shredded lemon peel, ½ cup lemon juice, ½ cup soft unsalted butter, and ¾ cup vanilla-infused superfine sugar (see Note) in a pan. Stir over low heat until all the sugar has dissolved. Lightly beat 4 egg yolks and slowly drizzle into the lemon mixture while stirring. Return the mixture to the heat and cook over low heat, stirring constantly, for about 5 minutes, or until thickened. Pour into clean, warm jars and seal while hot. Keep in the refrigerator for up to 2 months. Makes 1½ cups.

note TO MAKE VANILLA SUGAR, STORE A WHOLE VANILLA BEAN WITH THE SUPERFINE SUGAR IN AN AIRTIGHT CONTAINER FOR AT LEAST 1 WEEK PRIOR TO USE. REMOVE THE VANILLA BEAN BEFORE USE. IF WASHED AND DRIED THOROUGHLY, AND STORED IN AN AIRTIGHT CONTAINER, THE VANILLA BEAN CAN BE REUSED THREE OR FOUR TIMES.

STRAWBERRY CURD

Hull 1⅔ cups strawberries, then chop roughly and put in pan with ¾ cup superfine sugar, ½ cup soft unsalted butter, 1 tablespoon lemon juice, and 1 teaspoon shredded lemon peel. Stir over a low heat until the butter has melted and the sugar dissolved. Simmer gently for 5 minutes, then remove from the heat. Lightly beat 4 egg yolks in a large bowl, then slowly drizzle them into the strawberry mixture while stirring. The mixture will thicken as you add it. Return to low heat and then cook for 2 minutes while stirring. Do not allow the mixture to boil or the curd will separate. Pour into clean, warm jars and seal while hot. Keep in the refrigerator for up to 2 months. Makes 2 cups.

DRIED APRICOT CURD

Place ⅔ cup finely chopped dried apricots in a bowl, cover with ½ cup boiling water, and stand for 30 minutes. Stir to form a lumpy paste. Beat 4 eggs well and strain into a heatproof bowl, stir in ½ cup lemon juice, ½ cup superfine sugar, ¾ cup soft unsalted butter, and the apricot paste. Place the bowl over a pan of simmering water, without touching the water. Stir until the butter has melted and the sugar has dissolved. Stir constantly for about 15–20 minutes, or until the mixture thickly coats the back of a spoon. Spoon into clean, warm jars and seal while hot. Keep in the refrigerator for up to 2 months. Makes 2½ cups.

Microwave jams

These recipes are based on an 850-watt microwave. If your microwave wattage is different, cooking times may vary. Take extra care when cooking jams in a microwave, due to the extreme heat.

APRICOT JAM
Put two small plates in the freezer. Halve and remove the pits from 8 medium fresh apricots and roughly chop. Place in a microwave-proof bowl with 2 tablespoons lemon juice. Place the white pith from 1 lemon on a square of cheesecloth, then tie securely with string and place in the bowl. Cook, uncovered, on high for 6 minutes, stirring once or twice. Cool slightly, then measure. Add 1 cup sugar for every cup of fruit mixture and stir until all the sugar has dissolved. Cook, uncovered, on high for 15–20 minutes, or until the mixture reaches setting point. Test for setting point a couple of times during cooking (see page 8). If ready, discard the bag. Carefully pour the very hot (185°F) jam into clean, warm jars and seal. Turn the jars upside down for 2 minutes, then invert and let cool. Label and date. Makes 2 cups.

STRAWBERRY JAM
Put two small plates in the freezer. Hull and quarter 5 cups fresh strawberries and place in a microwave-proof bowl with ¼ cup lemon juice. Place the white pith from 1 lemon on a square of cheesecloth, then tie securely with string and place in the bowl. Cook, uncovered, on high for 6 minutes, or until the mixture is soft and pulpy, stirring once or twice. Cool slightly then measure. Add 1 cup sugar for every cup of fruit mixture and stir until the sugar has dissolved. Cook, uncovered, on high for 15–20 minutes, or until the mixture reaches setting point. Test for setting point during cooking (see page 8). When the jam is ready, discard the bag. Carefully pour the very hot (185°F) jam into clean, warm jars and seal. Turn the jars upside down for 2 minutes, then invert and let cool. Label and date. Makes 2 cups.

DRIED FIG JAM
Put two small plates in freezer. Remove the stalks from 2¾ cups dried figs and place in a microwave-proof bowl with 1½ cups water and 2 tablespoons lemon juice. Place the white pith from 1 lemon on a square of cheesecloth, tie securely with string and place in bowl. Cook, uncovered, on high for 10 minutes, or until the mixture is soft and pulpy, stirring once or twice. Cool slightly then measure. Add 1 cup sugar for every cup of fruit mixture and stir until all the sugar has dissolved. Cook, uncovered, on high for 15–20 minutes, or until the mixture reaches setting point. Test for setting point a couple of times during cooking (see page 12). Discard the bag. Carefully pour the very hot (185°F) jam into clean, warm jars and seal. Turn the jars upside down for 2 minutes, then invert and let cool. Label and date. Makes 4 cups.

CITRUS MARMALADE

Put two small plates in the freezer. Remove the peel from a grapefruit, a lemon, and an orange. Remove the pith and roughly chop the flesh. Remove the seeds. Place the pith and seeds onto a square of cheesecloth and tie securely with string. Place the peel and the bag in a microwave-proof bowl and cover with 1½ cups water. Cook, uncovered, on high for 10 minutes, or until the peel is soft. Cool slightly, then measure. Add 1 cup sugar for every cup of the fruit mixture and stir until dissolved. Cook, uncovered, on high for 20–25 minutes, or until the mixture reaches setting point. Test for setting point a couple of times during cooking (see page 8). Discard the bag. Carefully pour the very hot (185°F) jam into clean, warm jars and seal. Turn the jars upside down for 2 minutes, then invert and let cool. Label and date. Makes 2 cups.

MIXED BERRY JAM

Put two small plates in the freezer. Place 5 cups mixed berries in a microwave-proof bowl with ¼ cup lemon juice. Place the white pith from 1 lemon onto a square of cheesecloth, then tie securely with string and place in the bowl. Cook, uncovered, on high for 6 minutes or until the mixture is soft and pulpy, stirring once or twice. Cool slightly then measure. Add 1 cup sugar for every cup of fruit mixture and stir until all the sugar has dissolved. Cook, uncovered, on high for 15–20 minutes, or until the mixture reaches setting point. Test for setting point a couple of times during cooking (see page 8). If ready, discard the bag. Carefully pour the very hot (185°F) jam into clean, warm jars and seal. Turn the jars upside down for 2 minutes, then invert and let cool. Label and date. Makes 2 cups.

RASPBERRY JAM

Put two small plates in freezer. Place 5 cups raspberries in a microwave-proof bowl with ¼ cup lemon juice. Place the white pith from 1 lemon onto a square of cheesecloth, then tie securely with string and place in the bowl. Cook, uncovered, on high for 6 minutes, or until the mixture is soft and pulpy, stirring once or twice. Cool slightly and measure. Add 1 cup sugar for every cup of fruit mixture and stir until all the sugar has dissolved. Cook, uncovered, on high for 15–20 minutes, or until the mixture reaches setting point. Test for setting point a couple of times during cooking (see page 8). Discard the bag. Carefully pour the very hot (185°F) jam into clean, warm jars and seal. Turn the jars upside down for 2 minutes, then invert and let cool. Label and date. Makes 2 cups.

Liqueur fruits

Served over ice cream, with ricotta cheese or mascarpone, with brioche or panettone, or over toasted waffles or crêpes, these luscious, decadent liqueur fruits make an ideal finale to any meal. Make sure the fruit you use is just ripe and free of blemishes. Liqueur fruits should be left for a month before using to allow the flavors to develop and they must be refrigerated after opening.

APRICOTS IN RUM

Place ¾ cup sugar in a pan with 2 cups water. Stir over low heat until the sugar has dissolved. Bring to a boil, add 3¼ cups dried apricots, then reduce the heat and simmer for 3 minutes. Remove the pan from the heat and stir in ¾ cup dark rum. Make sure the temperature is at least 185°F and spoon into a clean, warm 4-cup capacity jar. Seal while hot and let cool. Label and date. Leave for 1 month before using. Store in a cool, dry place for 6 months. Makes 4 cups.

note IT IS VERY IMPORTANT TO USE A GOOD-QUALITY RUM FOR THIS RECIPE AS IT WILL DRASTICALLY AFFECT THE FLAVOR.

PRUNES IN PORT

Place ½ cup water, ⅓ cup sugar, and 8 cloves into a large pan. Stir over low heat until the sugar has dissolved. Bring to a boil, then reduce the heat and simmer for 15 minutes. Add 3 cups pitted prunes, thinly sliced peel of 1 orange, and about 2 cups port. Make sure the temperature is at least 185°F and spoon into a 4-cup capacity clean, warm jar. Seal while hot and let cool. Label and date. Leave for 1 month before using. Store in a cool, dry place for 6 months. Makes 4 cups.

note THE PRUNES WILL SWELL DURING STANDING.

MUSCAT FRUITS

Place ⅔ cup prunes, ¾ cup small dried figs, stems removed, 1 cup dried sliced apples, ¾ cup dried peach halves, 1 cup dried apricot halves, heaping ½ cup raisins, 2 strips orange peel, 2 cinnamon sticks, halved, 4 whole cloves, and 3 cups clear apple juice in a large nonmetallic bowl. Cover and soak overnight. Place in a large pan and bring to a boil, then reduce the heat and simmer for 5 minutes. Remove the pan from the heat and stir in 1 cup liqueur muscat. Make sure the temperature is at least 185°F and spoon the fruit mixture and syrup into clean, warm, wide-neck jars. Seal, label and date. Leave for 1 month before using. Store in a cool, dark place for 6 months. Makes about 4½ cups.

PRESERVED FIGS IN BRANDY

Place 3 cups sugar in a pan along with 1½ cups water. Stir over low heat until all the sugar has dissolved. Bring to a boil, then reduce heat, add 8 medium firm fresh figs and simmer for 5 minutes, or until the figs begin to soften (this will depend on ripeness of the figs). Lift the figs from the syrup with a slotted spoon, allowing as much syrup as possible to drain off and place them in clean, warm, wide-neck jars. Repeat with the remaining figs. Gently shake the jars to help settle the figs. Some syrup will accumulate in jars, so place the slotted spoon over the mouth of the jars and tip the excess syrup back into the pan. Bring the syrup to a boil and boil for 10 minutes, or until it thickens. Remove from the heat, allow any bubbles to subside, then pour 1½ cups of the syrup into a large heatproof jug, reserving any remaining syrup. Stir in 1½ cups brandy and pour into the jars to cover the figs. If there is not enough brandy syrup to cover, combine small quantities of the reserved syrup and some of the brandy in a jug and cover the figs. Make sure the temperature is at least 185°F and seal while hot. Label and store for 1 month before using. Store in a cool, dry place for 6 months. Refrigerate after opening. Makes 4 cups.

PEACHES IN BRANDY

Place 6–8 firm ripe slipstone peaches in a large bowl, cover with boiling water, then leave for 30 seconds. Remove the peaches using a slotted spoon and refresh in a bowl of icy water. Remove the skins, then cut the peaches in half and gently twist and pull apart to remove the pits. Place 1 cup water and ½ cup sugar in a large pan, and stir over low heat until all the sugar has dissolved. Bring to a boil, add the peach halves and simmer for 2–3 minutes. Remove the peaches with a slotted spoon and place into a 4-cup capacity clean, warm jar. Add a split vanilla bean to the syrup and simmer for 5 minutes. Stir in 1 cup brandy, then, making sure the temperature is at least 185°F, pour the syrup over the peaches, placing the vanilla bean inside the jar. Ensure that the fruit is fully covered with the syrup, leaving a very small space at the top of the jar. Seal and label. Leave for 2 weeks before using. Store in a cool, dry place for up to 6 months. Makes 4 cups.

Fruit pastes

Fruit pastes are a delicious method for preserving an overabundance of fruit. They may take a while to cook, but they keep for well for up to a year because of their high concentration of sugar. They are delicious served with coffee, as part of a cheeseboard, or with cold meats.

QUINCE PASTE

Line a 11 x 7-inch pan with baking parchment. Peel and core 10 (about 4½ pounds) small quinces, reserving the cores. Cut into chunks and place in a large pan. Chop the cores, place on a square of cheesecloth, then tie securely with string and add to the pan along with 2 cups water and 2 tablespoons lemon juice. Cook, covered, over low heat for 30–40 minutes, or until soft and tender. Cool slightly, then squeeze any juices from the bag and discard it. Purée the fruit in a blender or food processor until smooth, then press through a fine strainer. Weigh the purée and return it to the pan. Gradually add an equivalent measure of sugar. Stir over low heat, without boiling, until the sugar has dissolved. Cook, stirring with a wooden spoon to prevent from sticking and burning, for 45–60 minutes, or until the mixture leaves side of pan and is difficult to push the wooden spoon through.

APRICOT PASTE

Line a 11 x 7-inch pan with baking parchment. Select 30 (about 4½ pounds) medium apricots (you will need some to be a little green to help gel the paste). Remove the stalks, pits, and any blemishes. Cut the apricots into quarters and the remainder in half. Place in a large pan with 1 cup water and 2 tablespoons lemon juice. Bring to a boil, then reduce the heat and simmer, covered, for 15–20 minutes, or until the fruit is soft and tender. Cool slightly. Purée the fruit in a blender or food processor until smooth, then press through a fine strainer. Weigh the purée and return it to the pan. Gradually add an equivalent measure of sugar. Stir over low heat, without boiling, until all the sugar has dissolved. Cook, stirring with a wooden spoon to prevent sticking and burning, for 45–60 minutes, or until mixture leaves the side of the pan and it is difficult to push the wooden spoon through. (If the mixture starts to stick to the bottom of the pan, transfer it to a heatproof bowl, clean the pan, then return the mixture to the clean pan to continue cooking.)

PLUM PASTE

Line a 11 x 7-inch pan with baking parchment. Select 20 (3 pounds) medium plums (you will need some to be a little green to help gel the paste). Remove the stalks, pits, and any blemishes, then cut into quarters. Place in a large pan with 1 cup water and 2 tablespoons lemon juice. Bring to a boil, then reduce the heat and simmer, covered, for 20–30 minutes, or until the fruit is soft and tender. Cool slightly. Purée the fruit in a blender or food processor until smooth, then press through a fine strainer. Weigh the purée and return it to the pan. Gradually add an equal measure of sugar. Stir constantly over low heat, without boiling, until all the sugar has dissolved. Cook, stirring with a wooden spoon to prevent from sticking and burning, for 45–60 minutes, or until the mixture leaves the side of pan and is hard to push the wooden spoon through. (If the mixture starts to stick to the bottom of the pan, transfer it to a heatproof bowl, then clean the pan and return the mixture to the clean pan to continue the cooking.)

PEACH PASTE

Line a 11 x 7-inch pan with baking parchment. Remove the stalks, blemishes and pits from 13 (4½ pounds) medium peaches (you will need some to be a little green to help gel the paste). Cut each peach into 8 pieces and place in a large pan with 1 cup water and 3 tablespoons lemon juice. Bring to a boil, reduce heat and simmer, covered, for 20–30 minutes, or until the fruit is soft and tender. Cool slightly. Pureé the fruit in a blender or food processor until it is smooth, then press through a fine strainer. Weigh the purée and return it to the pan. Gradually add an equal measure of the sugar to the pan. Stir constantly over low heat, without boiling, until all the sugar has dissolved. Cook, stirring with a wooden spoon to prevent from sticking and burning, for 45–60 minutes, or until the mixture leaves the side of the pan and it is difficult to push the wooden spoon through. (If the mixture starts to stick to the bottom of pan, transfer it to a heatproof bowl, then clean the pan and return the mixture to the clean pan to continue cooking.)

TO PACKAGE AND STORE THE PASTES:

Spread into the prepared pan and smooth with a palette knife. Cut the pastes into small squares, diamonds, or triangles with a hot knife. Place a blanched almond in the center of each piece or roll in superfine sugar to coat, if desired. Wrap in foil and store in an airtight container in a cool, dry place. Disposable foil pans are ideal for storing fruit pastes. Spread the hot fruit mixture into them and press a piece of parchment paper onto the mixture before wrapping.

note AS THE MIXTURE THICKENS, IT WILL START TO SPLATTER. MAKE SURE YOU USE A LARGE, DEEP-SIDED PAN AND WRAP A DISH TOWEL AROUND YOUR HAND WHILE STIRRING.

Heat processing

Make the most of the abundance of fruit available each season and preserve them to be enjoyed for up to a year later. They will only keep for up to a week in the refrigerator, once opened.

Use either bottling jars with glass lids, spring clips, and rubber seals, or Kilner bottles with metal lids and rubber seals. Ensure the bottles fit snugly into the pot and will be fully submerged in the simmering water.

TEN STEPS TO HEAT PROCESSING

1   Choose just ripe or slightly underripe fruit, without blemishes.

2   Thoroughly wash and dry the bottles.

3   Pack the fruit tightly to allow for shrinkage during processing.

4   Dip the rubber seals into boiling water to sterilize them before placing them on the bottles.

5   To make the sugar syrup, place the sugar and water in a pan. Stir over low heat until dissolved. Brush the sides of the pan with a wet pastry brush to remove any undissolved sugar. Bring to the boil, and boil for 3 minutes.

6   Cover the fruit with hot syrup (185°F). Tap the bottles while filling to remove any air bubbles.

7   Carefully close the lids.

8   Put a folded dish towel on the base of the stockpot. Fill the pot with warm water (100°F) to submerge the bottles.

9   Gradually bring the water to simmering (190–194°C), this may take 25–30 minutes, then simmer steadily for the processing time. Do not allow the water to boil. Check the water level regularly and top up with boiling water, if required.

10 When processing is complete, remove the pot from the heat and remove some water. Wear rubber gloves or use tongs to remove the bottles. Do not put any pressure on lids. Place on a wooden board and cool overnight. Label and date.

To test that the seals on the spring-clip bottles are secure, release the clip and, with your fingertips, grip the rim of the lid and carefully lift the bottles. The seals will hold their own weight if properly processed. If they do not, store in the refrigerator and consume within 2 days.

PEARS

Mix 4 cups water with 1 teaspoon salt and 1 tablespoon lemon juice or ½ teaspoon citric acid in a large bowl. Peel 12 medium Bosc pears, then halve them and remove their cores. Place each pear in the lemon water mixture. Make a sugar syrup by dissolving 3 cups sugar in 6 cups boiling water and 1½ teaspoons citric acid or ¼ cup lemon juice. Arrange fruit in six 2-cup capacity bottles. Follow the 10 steps to heat processing. Cook for 30 minutes.

APRICOTS AND PLUMS

Score a cross in the base of 40 medium apricots or 30 medium plums. Place in a heatproof bowl and cover with boiling water. Leave for 30 seconds, then transfer to cold water. Peel away the skins, then halve and remove the pits. Make a sugar syrup by dissolving 2 cups sugar in 4 cups boiling water. Arrange the fruit in six 2-cup capacity bottles. Follow the 10 steps to heat processing. Cook for 15 minutes.

PEACHES

Score a cross in the base of 15 medium slipstone peaches. Place in a heatproof bowl and cover with boiling water. Leave for 30 seconds, then transfer to cold water. Remove the skins, then halve and remove the pits. Cut into ½-inch slices. Make a sugar syrup by dissolving 1½ cups sugar in 4½ cups boiling water. Arrange the fruit in six 2-cup capacity bottles. Follow the 10 steps to heat processing. Cook for 15 minutes.

TOMATOES

Score a cross in the base of 20 medium plum tomatoes. Place in a heatproof bowl and cover with boiling water. Leave for 30 seconds, then transfer the tomatoes to cold water and peel away the skins. Make a brine of 4½ teaspoons salt , 1 tablespoon citric acid, and 6 cups water. Stir to dissolve over low heat for 2–3 minutes. Arrange the tomatoes in six 2-cup bottles. Follow then 10 steps to heat processing, using the brine instead of sugar syrup. Cook for 20 minutes.

Index

Thunder Bay Press
An imprint of the Baker & Taylor Publishing Group
10350 Barnes Canyon Road, San Diego, CA 92121
www.thunderbaybooks.com

©Text and photography Murdoch Books Pty Limited 2005. ©Design Murdoch Books Pty Limited 2010.

All notations of errors or omissions should be addressed to Thunder Bay Press, Editorial Department, at the above address. All other correspondence (author inquiries, permissions) concerning the content of this book should be addressed to Murdoch Books Pty Limited, Pier 8/9, 23 Hickson Road, Sydney NSW 2000, Australia.

Cataloging-in publication information available upon request.

ISBN-13: 978-1-60710-298-4
ISBN-10: 1-60710-298-6

Printed in China

1 2 3 4 5 15 14 13 12 11